MOLIÈRE

THE MIDDLE-CLASS GENTLEMAN

Le Bourgeois Gentilhomme

TRANSLATION AND INTRODUCTION

BY HERMA BRIFFAULT

At first produced in 1670, the ballet-interludes were arranged and orchestrated by LULLY.

BARRON'S EDUCATIONAL SERIES, INC.

Woodbury, N. Y.

A Literal Translation of Le Bourgeois Gentilhomme by Molière

Translated by Herma Briffault

All inquiries should be addressed to
Barron's Educational Series, Inc.
113 Crossways Park Drive
Woodbury, New York 11797

PRINTED IN THE UNITED STATES OF AMERICA

6 7 8 9 10 11 M 10 9 8

INTRODUCTION

Le Bourgeois Gentilhomme was composed at the command of Louis XIV of France as an entertainment for a royal festival. It was first performed on October 14, 1670, at Chambord, where the court was then sojourning, and was liked so much by the noble audience that it was repeated three times for them in the following week. Molière himself esteemed it sufficiently to stage it at his theatre (then called the Théâtre du Palais-Royal) in the following month and to allow it to be published—a proceeding he rarely allowed with the light entertainments written by command for the royal festivals at Versailles, St.-Germain, and Chambord. Time has justified these original judgments for today, after an interval of almost four hundred years, this hilarious "comedy-ballet" is one of the most popular of the works of Molière; it still holds delight even when played in wretched translations and even when shorn of the musical interludes which Lully composed and which are an intrinsic part of the entertainment.

Although it satirizes the fashions, foibles, shams and snobberies of the period and pokes fun at middleclass people who think that, by aping gentlefolk and by denying the shameful fact that they and their ancestors are and were tradesmen, they can attain the status of the leisure class, this is not a "comedy of manners" to be judged by the standards we apply to Molière's *L'Ecole des femmes, Les Précieuses Ridicules, Tartuffe,* and *Le Misanthrope*—to name a few of his many great comedies of manners. For *Le Bourgeois Gentilhomme* has practically no plot and no character development: here, wild exaggeration and caricature are the rule and the object is purely to entertain. It is a show with music, as topical in its time as the musical shows of Gilbert and Sullivan in the 19th century, and the shows of Rodgers and Hammerstein in our own century. The extremely colloquial dialogue is fast-paced, and obviously meant to correspond to the fast-paced rhythms of the music which the court orchestra leader, Jean-Baptiste Lully, had evolved for the interludes of this entertainment and several others which Molière had written for royal festivals. The intervals are a part of the entertainment; the dialogue is enhanced by the songs and dances that interlard it; to produce *Le Bourgeois Gentilhomme* as straight comedy, shorn of these adornments, is to miss much of its point.

Nearly all of the court entertainments arranged by Molière for Louis XIV, who had subsidized his theatre in 1661 and who defended him against the enemies his satirical comedies earned him throughout his lifetime, were written in collaboration with some musician or versifier.

His first such entertainment, *Les Fàcheux* (misleadingly entitled *The Impertinents* in English) was composed in collaboration with the great poet La Fontaine for a fastuous reception given by the Minister of Finance, Fouquet, to the King in 1661 (Fouquet's last great show of wealth, for he was arrested and imprisoned for embezzlement shortly afterwards) and the hunting scene in it was suggested by the King himself. In collaboration with Lully, Molière composed *Le Mariage Forcé* for a royal festival at Versailles in 1664, and the King himself danced in it. Lully also furnished the music and dances for *Monsieur de Pourceaugnac* which was presented at a royal festival at Chambord in 1669. *Le Bourgeois Gentilhomme* must be compared with these light entertainments to discover its superiorities, for it is without any doubt the best composition in this category that issued from Molière's brain; and is likewise the most personal as well as the most popular.

Of ironic interest is the fact that this entertainment commanded by France's greatest gentleman, King Louis XIV, for the diversion of his court, was composed by two great members of the *bourgeoise*: both Jean-Baptiste Lully and Jean-Baptiste Poquelin (Molière's real name) were of the tradesman-class. Lully's father was a tanner in Florence; Molière's father, Jean Poquelin, was an upholsterer. Molière's baptismal certificate, dated January 15, 1622, and registered in the parish of St. Eustache, Paris, informs us that Jean Poquelin was *valet de chambre, tapissier du roi,* upholsterer employed in the royal household. It is also known that Molière was to succeed his father in this post and actually held it briefly, in 1642. Fortunately for French comedy and the literature of the world, Molière turned his back upon that *bourgeois* career in 1642, joining a theatrical troupe headed by Madeleine Béjart and touring the provinces for the next fifteen years. When he returned to Paris he was introduced to the court by the Prince de Conti, who had remarked his talent as an actor, and from that time onward he was an honored figure at court, having the King's most sincere protection.

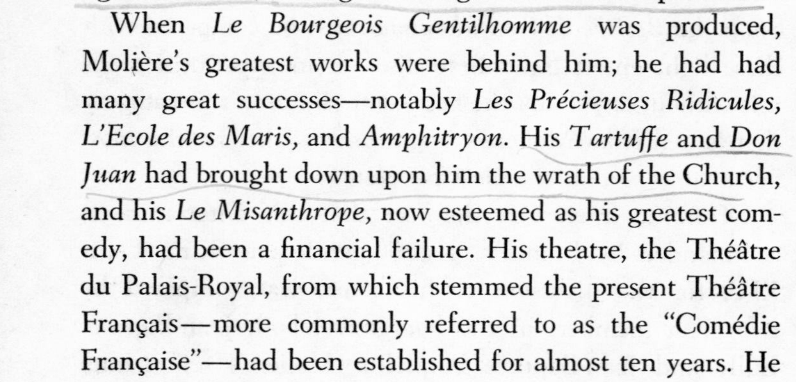

When *Le Bourgeois Gentilhomme* was produced, Molière's greatest works were behind him; he had had many great successes—notably *Les Précieuses Ridicules, L'Ecole des Maris,* and *Amphitryon.* His *Tartuffe* and *Don Juan* had brought down upon him the wrath of the Church, and his *Le Misanthrope,* now esteemed as his greatest comedy, had been a financial failure. His theatre, the Théâtre du Palais-Royal, from which stemmed the present Théâtre Français—more commonly referred to as the "Comédie Française"—had been established for almost ten years. He was at an age (forty-eight) that we now consider the prime of life, but he was aged prematurely by an illness that was to end in death three years later. Only one great comedy remained to be written by him: *Le Malade Imaginaire,* a satire on the medical profession, written while he was a dying man, and in which he acted right up to the end, since he was carried home to die after a performance of that play on February 17, 1673.

The exact location of his tomb is not known; we do know that he died without absolution and that, had the King not intervened, Molière would have been buried, according to the regulations of the time, in unconsecrated ground. We know that he was buried in the cemetery of St. Eustache, but without church ceremony. And that is all.

But Molière's works remain, and they are the best explanation of his life. He was a man who loved life—and laughed at it. He wielded a veritable rapier of wit—but the tip of the rapier was never poisoned. He could laugh at himself as well as at others, but never with the bitterness that leaves a bad taste in the mouth. And when, as in the absurdly exaggerated character of Monsieur Jourdain, he laughs at his own background, he is still, by some subtle magic, able to make us forgive Monsieur Jourdain his absurdities, even while laughing at them. Perhaps it is this great humanity of Molière that has given his plays their enduring power to move us. All were topical—that is to say timely—and all have proved to be timeless; none more so than *Le Bourgeois Gentilhomme*.

We continue, by preference, to use the French title for this comedy-ballet, because there is no title that fully conveys its meaning to an American mind. In the United States, where there has never been a royal court, there has been no true aristocracy or upperclass, and therefore no true middleclass. To be a tradesman in the United States has never caused anyone to be shut out of a privileged group—as it still does in present day England where many schools are shut to any but the sons and daughters of "gentlemen"—a gentleman being a member of the upper or leisure class. In the United States the term "citizen" has always been held to be most honorable; whereas in England and France, at least down to the 19th century, the word described all those outside court circles; it was the pendant to courtier. "The Middleclass Gentleman" is, however, a literal translation of the French title, and we have used it for our translation, while still feeling that "The Would-be Gentleman" is a more descriptive title in the United States. In recent years, however, the word "bourgeois" has entered the English language, so that the original title might very well be kept, since it defies translation and, with its contradiction in terms (it is of course impossible to be a "middleclass gentleman" since "gentleman" means a member of the upper-class) contains the germ of all the laughter of the play.

The play itself has never been adequately translated: the 18th century translation generally used is very weak in its rendering of French idioms, turning them into stiff and literary expressions, transposing words and phrases still in current French use into words and phrases that are archaic or obsolete in English.[1] Our present translation has tried to capture something of the colloquial flavor of the original, while remaining close to the French text, and it may be hoped it will be useful as a crutch to the feeble beginner in the French language. But to appreciate Molière fully—his brisk pace, his sure ear for spoken language, his keen wit—he must be read in the French language he helped to mould. To translate any great author is to betray him, as the Italians put it in a proverb, and the greater the author the greater the betrayal. In the same way, to effect cuts in a piece by a great author is to commit a sacrilege, since it misconstrues the original intention. This is particularly so with *Le Bourgeois Gentilhomme,* which is too often deprived of its song-and-dance interludes. Let us now glance at these, and discover how topical they are, how intrinsic a part of the original entertainment.

The First Interlude is a parody of the literary form of the Pastoral, then much in vogue—Molière himself had written one for a royal festival. The Second Interlude pokes fun at the fashions which were then reaching in both male

---

[1] *Note. See the 18th century translation published in Everyman's Library, where, for examples of this, "bonne chère" is rendered as "good cheer"; "rien à faire" as "no more dealings" "mêlez-vous de vos affaires" as "meddle you with your own affairs." The French phrases are still current; we have rendered them, in our translation into words still current: "good viads," "nothing doing," "mind your own business," which is closer to the original and is not archaic.*

and female attire a state of exaggerated adornment never equalled before or since. The Third Interlude satirizes the then growing refinements of French *cuisine* and the fashionable gourmets who talked endlessly about food in a very special jargon. The Fourth Interlude, and the most hilarious, is likewise the most topical, since only the previous year an emissary of the Sultan of the Ottoman Empire had visited the French court and had made himself thoroughly detested; it was by Louis XIV's request that this Turkish interlude was inserted. The Fifth Interlude, which we have not translated, is merely a grand finale, celebrating, through love-songs in three languages—French, Spanish, and Italian—some recently negotiated treaties that had been signed by the King, for whom this masterly entertainment was written.

HERMA BRIFFAULT

CHARACTERS

MONSIEUR JOURDAIN, the "middle-class gentleman,"
MADAME JOURDAIN, his wife,
LUCILE, their daughter,
NICOLE, their maid-servant,
CLÉONTE, Lucile's suitor,
COVIELLE, Cléonte's valet,
DORANTE, Count, in love with Dorimène,
DORIMÈNE, Marchioness,
MUSIC-MASTER,
PUPIL OF MUSIC-MASTER,
DANCING-MASTER,
FENCING-MASTER,
PHILOSOPHY-MASTER,
MASTER-TAILOR,
APPRENTICE-TAILOR,
TWO LACKEYS, in attendance upon Monsieur Jourdain,
Musicians and singers (male and female), and a Corps de Ballet for the various Interludes.

SCENE: Monsieur Jourdain's house in Paris, and its approaches.

ACT ONE

SCENE I

The play opens with a great assembling of instruments. Working at a table, centre-stage, we see a Pupil of the Music-Master, composing a melody which the would-be Gentleman, Monsieur Jourdain, has ordered for a serenade.

MUSIC-MASTER: *(To musicians).* Come, come into this hall, sit there and wait till he comes.

DANCING-MASTER: *(To dancers).* And you too, on this side.

MUSIC-MASTER: *(To pupil).* Is it done?

PUPIL: Yes.

MUSIC-MASTER: Let's see . . . This is good.

DANCING-MASTER: Is it something new?

MUSIC-MASTER: Yes, 'tis a melody for a serenade that I set him to composing here, while waiting for our goodman to awake.

DANCING-MASTER: May I see what it is?

MUSIC-MASTER: You'll hear it, with the dialogue, when he comes. He'll not be very long in coming.

DANCING-MASTER: Our work's not paltry, yours and mine, at present.

MUSIC-MASTER: That's true. We've found here such a man as we both need. A pleasant revenue for us is this Monsieur Jourdain, with his visions of nobility and gallantry which he's got into his head. Both your dancing and my music could hope that everyone resembled him!

DANCING-MASTER: Not entirely; and I could wish for him that he were a better judge than he is in the things we give him.

MUSIC-MASTER: 'Tis true he understands them illy, but he pays well for them. And, for the moment, that's what our art needs more than anything.

DANCING-MASTER: As for me, I'll avow it to you, I feed on glory just a little. Applause touches me, and I hold that, in all the fine-arts, it's a very tiresome torment to produce for blockheads, to endure the barbarous judgment of a fool upon our compositions. It's a pleasure, say no more on't, to work for persons capable of feeling the fine points of an art; who know how to give an agreeable reception to the beauties of a work and, by pleasurable approbations, gratify us for our labor. Yes, the most agreeable recompense we can receive for the things we do is to see them recognized and flattered by applause that honors us. In my opinion, nothing repays us better than that for all our strains; and the praises of the well-informed are exquisite delights.

MUSIC-MASTER: I agree with all that, and I enjoy them as you do. Assuredly, there's nothing more pleasurable than the applause you speak of; but that incense does not support life. Unmixed praises do not place a man in easy circumstances; something solid must be added, and the best way to praise is with open hands. He's a man, 'tis true, whose enlightenments are very paltry, who talks without rhyme or reason on everything and who applauds only for the wrong reason. But his money rectifies his judgments. He has discernment in his purse. His praises are minted coin; and this ignorant burgher is worth more to us, as you see, than the educated nobleman who introduced us here.

DANCING-MASTER: There's some truth in what you say; but I find you lean a little too heavily on money; and material benefit is something so base that a man of good taste should never show an attachment for it.

MUSIC-MASTER: For all that, you take quite willingly the money our goodman gives you.

DANCING-MASTER: Assuredly. But I don't place all my happiness in it, and I could wish that along with his fortune he had some slight good taste in things.

MUSIC-MASTER: I could wish it too, and it is towards that end that we are working, we two, as much as possible. But in any case he gives us the means to make ourselves known in the world; and he will pay for the others what the others will praise for him.

DANCING-MASTER: Here he comes.

SCENE II

MONSIEUR JOURDAIN: Well, gentlemen? What's up? Are you going to show me your little skit?

DANCING-MASTER: How? What little skit?

MONSIEUR JOURDAIN: Well, the . . . What-you-may-call-it. Your prologue or dialogue of songs and dances.

DANCING-MASTER: Ha, ha!

MUSIC-MASTER: You find us ready for you.

MONSIEUR JOURDAIN: I kept you waiting a little, but it's because I'm having myself dressed today like the gentlefolk, and my tailor sent me some silk stockings that I thought I could never get on.

MUSIC-MASTER: We are here only to wait upon your leisure.

MONSIEUR JOURDAIN: I desire you both to stay until they have brought me my coat, so that you may see me.

DANCING-MASTER: Whatever you like.

MONSIEUR JOURDAIN: You will see me fitted out properly, from head to foot.

MUSIC-MASTER: We have no doubt of it.

MONSIEUR JOURDAIN: I had this Indienne cloth made for me.

DANCING-MASTER: 'Tis very handsome.

MONSIEUR JOURDAIN: My tailor told me the gentlefolk are like this of a morning.

MUSIC-MASTER: 'Tis marvellously becoming.

MONSIEUR JOURDAIN: Ho, there, lackeys! My two lackeys! (Enter: 2 Lackeys)

FIRST LACKEY: Your command, Sir?

MONSIEUR JOURDAIN: Nothing. 'Twas to see if you hear me well. *(To the two masters)*. What say you of my liveries?

DANCING-MASTER: They're magnificent.

MONSIEUR JOURDAIN: *(Half opening his gown, disclosing a pair of tight red velvet breeches, and a green velvet vest, which he is wearing).* Here again is a kind of lounging dress to perform my morning exercises in.

MUSIC-MASTER: 'Tis elegant.

MONSIEUR JOURDAIN: Lackey!

FIRST LACKEY: Sir?

MONSIEUR JOURDAIN: 'Tother lackey!

SECOND LACKEY: Sir?

MONSIEUR JOURDAIN: *(Taking off his gown).* Hold my gown. *(To the Masters).* Think you I look well so?

DANCING-MASTER: Very well. No one could look better.

MONSIEUR JOURDAIN: Now let's have a look at your thingumajig.

MUSIC-MASTER: First of all I would very much like for you to listen to a melody he has just composed for the serenade that you requested. He's one of my pupils who has an admirable talent for these kinds of things.

MONSIEUR JOURDAIN: Yes, but you should not have had that done by a pupil; you yourself were none too good for that piece of work.

MUSIC-MASTER: You must not let the name of pupil fool you, sir. Pupils of this sort know as much as the greatest masters, and the melody is as fine as could be made. But listen, now.

MONSIEUR JOURDAIN: *(To Lackeys)*. Give me my robe so I may listen better . . . Stay, I believe I would be better without a gown . . . No, give it me again, that will be better.

MUSICIAN: *(Singing)*.

I languish night and day, my suffering is extreme
Since to your hard rule your lovely eyes subjected me;
If you thus treat, fair Iris, those you love,
Alas, how would you treat an enemy?

MONSIEUR JOURDAIN: This song seems to me a little mournful, it lulls to sleep; I would that you might liven it up a little, here and there.

MUSIC-MASTER: Sir, the tune must be suited to the words.

MONSIEUR JOURDAIN: Some time ago I was taught a perfectly pretty one. Now . . . uh . . . how does it go?

DANCING-MASTER: By my troth, I know not.

MONSIEUR JOURDAIN: There's sheep in it.

DANCING-MASTER: Sheep?

MONSIEUR JOURDAIN: Yes. Oh! *(He sings)*.

I thought my Janneton
As beautiful as sweet;
I thought my Janneton
Far gentler than a sheep.
Alas! Alas!
She's crueller far,
A hundred times, a thousand times,
Than jungle-tigers are!

Ain't it pretty?

MUSIC-MASTER: The prettiest in the world.

DANCING-MASTER: And you sing it well.

MONSIEUR JOURDAIN: It's without having learned music.

MUSIC-MASTER: You ought to learn it, sir, as you are learning dancing. They are two arts which have a close connection.

DANCING-MASTER: And which open the mind of man to fine things.

MONSIEUR JOURDAIN: And do gentlefolk learn music, too?

MUSIC-MASTER: Yes sir.

MONSIEUR JOURDAIN: I'll learn it then. But I don't know when I could find time; for besides the fencing-master who's showing me, I have also retained a master of philosophy who is to begin this morning.

MUSIC-MASTER: Philosophy is something; but music, sir, music . . .

DANCING-MASTER: Music and dancing, music and dancing, that's all that's needed.

MUSIC-MASTER: There's nothing so useful to the State as music.

DANCING-MASTER: There's nothing so necessary to men as dancing.

MUSIC-MASTER: Without music, a State cannot subsist.

DANCING-MASTER: Without the dance, a man can do nothing.

MUSIC-MASTER: All the disorders, all the wars one sees in the world happen only from not learning music.

DANCING-MASTER: All the misfortunes of mankind, all the dreadful disasters that fill the history books, the blunders of politicians and the lapses of great commanders, all this proceeds from not knowing how to dance.

MONSIEUR JOURDAIN: How so?

MUSIC-MASTER: Does not war result from a lack of concord between men?

MONSIEUR JOURDAIN: That is true.

MUSIC-MASTER: And if all men learned music, would not that be a means of bringing harmony and of seeing universal peace in the world?

MONSIEUR JOURDAIN: You are right.

DANCING-MASTER: When a man has committed a default, either in family affairs or in affairs of government of a state, or in the commandment of an army, do we not always say, "He took a false step in such and such an affair?"

MONSIEUR JOURDAIN: Yes, that's said.

DANCING-MASTER: And can taking a false step result from anything but not knowing how to dance?

MONSIEUR JOURDAIN: 'Tis true, and you are both right.

DANCING-MASTER: It makes you see the excellence and usefulness of music and the dance.

MONSIEUR JOURDAIN: I understand that, now.

MUSIC-MASTER: Do you wish to see our things?

MONSIEUR JOURDAIN: Yes.

MUSIC-MASTER: I have already told you that it is a little

essay I made in the past upon the different passions that music can express.

MONSIEUR JOURDAIN: Very good.

MUSIC-MASTER *(To musicians)*. Here, come forward. *(To M. Jourdain)*. You must imagine that they are dressed as shepherds.

MONSIEUR JOURDAIN: Why always shepherds? You see nothing but that everywhere.

MUSIC-MASTER: When we have characters that are to speak in music, 'tis necessary, for probability, to go in for the pastoral, singing has always been assigned to shepherds. It is not at all natural in dialogue for princes or shopkeepers to sing their passions.

MONSIEUR JOURDAIN: Very good, very good. Let's see.

Dialogue in Music: (a Woman and Two Men.)

WOMAN:

A heart subjected to love's tyranny
is always with a thousand cares oppressed.
'Tis said we gladly languish, gladly sigh;
and yet despite what can be said,
There's naught so sweet as liberty!

FIRST MAN:

There's naught so sweet as the loving fires
that make two hearts subsist in one sole longing.
Happy we cannot be, deprived of amorous desires;
take love from life, you take away the pleasures.

SECOND MAN:

Sweet 'twould be to enter 'neath love's sway,
if one could find in love some constancy,
But oh, alas, oh ruthless rule!
no constant shepherdess do we see,
and that inconstant sex, far too unworthy,
should henceforth give up love eternally.

FIRST MAN:

Refreshing ardor!

WOMAN:

Refreshing liberty!

SECOND MAN:

Deceitful woman!

FIRST MAN:

How precious art thou to me!

WOMAN:

How pleasant art thou to my heart!

SECOND MAN:

How horrible art thou to me!

FIRST MAN:

Oh, leave, for love, that mortal hate!

WOMAN:

We can, we can display to you
a constant shepherdess!

SECOND MAN:

Alas—where find her?

WOMAN:

Our honor to retrieve,
my heart upon you I bestow!

FIRST MAN:

But, shepherdess, can I believe
that 'twill not be deceitful?

WOMAN:

We'll see, by trial,
who of the two loves best.

SECOND MAN:

May the gods destroy
whoever lackest constancy!

ALL THREE:

Now let us be inflamed
with fires so beautiful!
Oh, how sweet it is to love,
when two hearts are united!

MONSIEUR JOURDAIN: Is that all?

MUSIC-MASTER: Yes.

MONSIEUR JOURDAIN: I find 'tis well-despatched, and there are some pretty sayings in it.

DANCING-MASTER: Here, for my composition, is a little

essay of the loveliest movements and the most beautiful attitudes with which a dance can possibly be varied.

MONSIEUR JOURDAIN: Are these shepherds too?

DANCING-MASTER: They're whatever you like. *(To the dancers)* Come along!

(Four dancers execute all the different movements and all the kinds of steps that the Dancing-Master orders; and this dance comprises the First Interlude.)

ACT TWO

SCENE I

MONSIEUR JOURDAIN: That's not at all silly, and those fellows there jig up and down well.

MUSIC-MASTER: When the dance is mixed with the music, it will have still more effect, and you will see something gay in the little ballet we have arranged for you.

MONSIEUR JOURDAIN: Well, that's for by and by. And the person I ordered all this for is to do me the honor of dining here on the spot.

DANCING-MASTER: Everything is ready.

MUSIC-MASTER: However, sir, this is not enough. A person such as you, who live magnificently, and who are inclined towards fine things, should have a concert of music at your house every Wednesday or every Thursday.

MONSIEUR JOURDAIN: Why? Do gentlefolk have them?

MUSIC-MASTER: Yes, sir.

MONSIEUR JOURDAIN: Then I'll have 'em. Will it be fine?

MUSIC-MASTER: Undoubtedly. You must have three voices—a tenor, a soprano, and a bass, who will be accompanied by a bass-viol, a theorbo, and a clavecin for the chords, with two violins to play the little symphonies.

MONSIEUR JOURDAIN: You must also add a trumpet-marine. The trumpet-marine is an instrument that pleases me, and it's harmonious.

MUSIC-MASTER: Allow us to manage things.

MONSIEUR JOURDAIN: At least, don't forget to send the musicians by and by to sing at table.

MUSIC-MASTER: You will have everything you should have.

MONSIEUR JOURDAIN: But above all, let the ballet be fine.

MUSIC-MASTER: You will be pleased with it, and, among other things, with certain minuets you'll find in it.

MONSIEUR JOURDAIN: Oh! Minuets are my dance, and I have a mind that you should see me dance them. Come, my dancing-master.

DANCING-MASTER: A hat, sir, if you please! *(The footman hands him a plumed tricorne hat which, correctly, should be carried under the right arm, the head being covered only with its heavy perruque; but M. Jourdain claps the hat on top of his night-cap)* La, la-di-da, la, la. La, la, la, la-di-da. Don't move your shoulders so. La, la, la, la-di-da. . . . Your arms are out of joint. La, la, la, la-di-da, la, la, la, la, la, la. Raise your head. Turn the toe out. Straighten your body up.

MONSIEUR JOURDAIN: Heh? *(He is out of breath, but asking approval).*

MUSIC-MASTER: Most admirable!

MONSIEUR JOURDAIN: By the way, teach me how to salute a marchioness; I shall need to know by and by.

DANCING-MASTER: How you must bow to salute a marchioness?

MONSIEUR JOURDAIN: Yes, a marchioness who's called Dorimène.

DANCING-MASTER: Give me your hand.

MONSIEUR JOURDAIN: No. You have only to do it, I shall remember it well.

DANCING-MASTER: If you would salute her with a great deal of respect, you must first bow and step back, then walk towards her, bowing three times, and at the last one, you bow down to her knees.

MONSIEUR JOURDAIN: *(After the Dancing-Master has illustrated)* Do it a bit. Good!

LACKEY: Sir, your fencing-master: he is here.

MONSIEUR JOURDAIN: Bid him to come in here to teach. I want you to see me perform.

SCENE II

FENCING-MASTER: *(Giving a foil to M. Jourdain)*. Come, sir, the salute. Your body straight. A little inclined upon the left thigh. Your legs not so wide apart. Your feet both on a line. Your wrist opposite your hip. The point of your sword against your shoulder. The arm not so much extended. The left hand at the level of the eye. The left shoulder more squared. The head up. The expression, bold. Advance. The body steady. Beat carte, and push carte. One, two. Recover. Again, with the foot firm. One, two. Leap back. When you make a pass, sir, your sword must disengage first, and your body must be well effaced. One, two. Come, beat tierce, and push the same. Advance. The body firm. Advance. Quit after that manner. One, two. Recover. Repeat the same. One, two. Leap back. Parry, sir, parry! *(The fencing-master gives him two or three home thrusts, saying, "Parry!")*

MONSIEUR JOURDAIN: Heh? *(As in dancing-lesson, out of breath, but asking for admiration).*

MUSIC-MASTER: You perform wonders.

FENCING-MASTER: I have already told you: the whole secret of arms consists of only two things: to give and not to take. And, as I made you see the other day by demonstration, it is impossible for you to receive if you know how to turn your adversary's sword from the line of your body; which only depends upon a slight movement of the wrist, either inward or outward.

MONSIEUR JOURDAIN: In that way, then, a man without courage is sure to kill his man and not be killed at all?

FENCING-MASTER: No doubt of it. Did you not see the demonstration?

MONSIEUR JOURDAIN: Yes.

FENCING-MASTER: And by that you see in what consideration men like me should be held in the State, and how the science of arms excels greatly all other useless sciences, such as dancing, music, and . . .

DANCING-MASTER: Softly, softly, sir handler of arms. Don't speak of dancing except with respect.

MUSIC-MASTER: I pray you, learn to treat better the excellence of music.

FENCING-MASTER: Amusing folk, to want to compare your sciences with mine!

MUSIC-MASTER: Do but see the importance of the man!

FENCING-MASTER: My little dancing-master, I'll make you dance as you should! And you, my little musician, I'll make you sing in the prettiest way!

DANCING-MASTER: Mr. Bang-Bang on steel, I'll teach you your trade!

MONSIEUR JOURDAIN: *(To Dancing-Master).* Are you insane, to seek quarrel with him, who understands tierce and carte, and who knows how to kill a man by demonstration?

DANCING-MASTER: I spit at his demonstrative reason and at his tierce, and at his carte!

MONSIEUR JOURDAIN: Gently! Gently, I say.

FENCING-MASTER: What? Impertinent little creature!

MONSIEUR JOURDAIN: Hoh, my Fencing-Master!

DANCING-MASTER: *(To Fencing-Master)* What? You big dray-horse!

MONSIEUR JOURDAIN: Hoh, my Dancing-Master!

FENCING-MASTER: If I hurl myself at you . . .

MONSIEUR JOURDAIN: Gently!

DANCING-MASTER: If I lay my hands on you . . .

MONSIEUR JOURDAIN: Be nice!

FENCING-MASTER: I'll go over you with a curry-comb, in such a way . . .

MONSIEUR JOURDAIN: Mercy!

DANCING-MASTER: I'll give you a drubbing such as . . .

MONSIEUR JOURDAIN: I beg of you!

MUSIC-MASTER: Let us teach him a little how to talk!

MONSIEUR JOURDAIN: Oh, Lordy, stop!

SCENE III *(Master of Philosophy enters)*

MONSIEUR JOURDAIN: Hallo! Mr. Philosopher, you come in the nick of time with your philosophy. Come, make a little peace among these persons here.

PHILOSOPHY-MASTER: Why, what's happening? What's the matter, sirs?

MONSIEUR JOURDAIN: They have got into a rage over their professions, which is to be preferred; and to the point of injurious words and of wanting to come to blows.

PHILOSOPHY-MASTER: What, gentlemen! Must you fly into such a rage? Have you not read the learned treatise that Seneca composed upon anger? Is there anything baser and more shameful than this passion which turns a man into a savage beast? And should not reason be the mistress of all our activities?

DANCING-MASTER: Why, sir, he has just abused both of

us by despising the dance which is my profession and music, which is his profession.

PHILOSOPHY-MASTER: A wise man is above all the insults that can be spoken to him; and the grand reply we should make to such affronts is moderation and patience.

FENCING-MASTER: They both had the audacity to compare their professions with mine.

PHILOSOPHY-MASTER: Should that disturb you? Men should not dispute amongst themselves about vainglory and rank; that which perfectly distinguishes one from the other is wisdom and virtue.

DANCING-MASTER: I tell him emphatically that the dance is a science to which one cannot do enough honor.

MUSIC-MASTER: And I maintain that music is one that every epoch has revered.

FENCING-MASTER: And I affirm to both that the science of arms is the finest and the most necessary of all sciences.

PHILOSOPHY-MASTER: And where then will philosophy be? I consider you very impertinent, all three of you, to talk with this arrogance in front of me, and impudently to honor with the name of science things that should not even be honored with the name of art, and that cannot be classified except under the name of a pitiful trade—gladiator, singer, mountebank!

FENCING-MASTER: Get out, you dog of a philosopher!

MUSIC-MASTER: Get out, you scoundrel of a pedant!

DANCING-MASTER: Get out, you cad of a pedagogue!

PHILOSOPHY-MASTER: What! Villains that you are . . . *(The philosopher flings himself at them, and all three go out, fighting).*

MONSIEUR JOURDAIN: Sir Philosopher!

(They reappear, still fighting).

PHILOSOPHY-MASTER: Rogues! Scoundrels! Insolent curs!

MONSIEUR JOURDAIN: Sir Philosopher!

FENCING-MASTER: Plague take the animal!

MONSIEUR JOURDAIN: Gentlemen!

PHILOSOPHY-MASTER: Impudent villains!

MONSIEUR JOURDAIN: Sir Philosopher!

DANCING-MASTER: The devil take the stupid jack-ass!

MONSIEUR JOURDAIN: Gentlemen!

PHILOSOPHY-MASTER: Knaves!

MONSIEUR JOURDAIN: Sir Philosopher!

MUSIC-MASTER: The devil take the impertinent fellow!

MONSIEUR JOURDAIN: Gentlemen!

PHILOSOPHY-MASTER: Rascals! Ragamuffins! Traitors! Impostors! *(They go out).*

MONSIEUR JOURDAIN: Mr. Philosopher! Gentlemen! Mr. Philosopher! Gentlemen! Mr. Philosopher! Oh! Fight as you like, I'd not know what to do, and I'll not spoil my gown to separate you! I'd be a great fool to mix up with them and receive some blow that would hurt.

SCENE IV

PHILOSOPHY-MASTER: (*Entering and straightening the white collar that distinguishes him as a Philosopher*). Now to our lesson.

MONSIEUR JOURDAIN: Oh, Sir, I am vexed at the blows they gave you.

PHILOSOPHY-MASTER: 'Tis nothing at all. A philosopher knows how to take things and I'll compose a satire against them, in the manner of Juvenal, which will tear them to shreds. Let that pass. What do you wish to learn?

MONSIEUR JOURDAIN: Everything I can, for I have every desire in the world to be learned, and I'm furious that my father and mother did not make me study all the sciences when I was young.

PHILOSOPHY-MASTER: This is a reasonable sentiment. *Nam sine doctrina vita est quasi mortis imago*. You understand that, and you know Latin without doubt?

MONSIEUR JOURDAIN: Yes, but act as if I did not know it. Tell me what that says.

PHILOSOPHY-MASTER: It means to say that without science life is almost an image of death.

MONSIEUR JOURDAIN: That Latin is right.

PHILOSOPHY-MASTER: Do you know some principles, some rudiments of the sciences?

MONSIEUR JOURDAIN: Oh yes! I can read and write.

PHILOSOPHY-MASTER: Where would it please you for

us to begin? Would you like me to teach you logic?

MONSIEUR JOURDAIN: And just what is this logic?

PHILOSOPHY-MASTER: It is that which teaches the three operations of the mind.

MONSIEUR JOURDAIN: Who or what are those three operations of the mind?

PHILOSOPHY-MASTER: The first, the second, and the third. The first is to conceive well by means of the universals; the second is to judge well by means of the categories; and the third is to draw well a conclusion by means of figures. *Barbara, Celarent, Darii, Ferio, Baralipton, etc.*

MONSIEUR JOURDAIN: Now, there are words that are too crabbed. That logic there does not suit me at all. Let's learn something else that's prettier.

PHILOSOPHY-MASTER: Would you learn morality?

MONSIEUR JOURDAIN: Morality?

PHILOSOPHY-MASTER: Yes.

MONSIEUR JOURDAIN: What does it say, this morality?

PHILOSOPHY-MASTER: It treats of happiness, teaches men to moderate their passions, and . . .

MONSIEUR JOURDAIN: No, let's leave that. I'm as choleric as the devil and there's no morality that sticks, I want to get fit to burst with anger whenever I like.

PHILOSOPHY-MASTER: Would you learn physics?

MONSIEUR JOURDAIN: What's it up to, this physics?

PHILOSOPHY-MASTER: Physics is the science that explains the principles of natural things and the properties of the body; it discourses on the nature of the elements, of metals, of minerals, of stones, of plants and animals, and teaches us the causes of all the meteors, the rainbow, the will o' the wisps, the comets, lightning, thunder, thunderbolts, rain, snow, hail, winds, and whirlwinds.

MONSIEUR JOURDAIN: There's too much hurly-burly in that, too much commotion.

PHILOSOPHY-MASTER: Then what would you have me teach you?

MONSIEUR JOURDAIN: Teach me how to spell.

PHILOSOPHY-MASTER: Very gladly.

MONSIEUR JOURDAIN: Afterwards, you may teach me the almanack, to know when there is a moon and when not.

PHILOSOPHY-MASTER: So be it. Following your thought well and treating this matter in the manner of a philosopher, we must begin according to the order of things, by an exact knowledge of the nature of letters and the different ways of pronouncing them all. And thereupon I must tell you that letters are divided into vowels, called vowels because they express the voice; and into consonants because they sound with the vowels and only mark the diverse articulations of the voice. There are five vowels or voices: A, E, I, O, U.[1]

MONSIEUR JOURDAIN: I understand all that.

PHILOSOPHY-MASTER: The vowel A is formed by widely opening the mouth: A.

---

[1] *The vowels are to be given the sounds used in vocalizing: Ah-aye-ee-o-ou.*

MONSIEUR JOURDAIN: A, A, yes.

PHILOSOPHY-MASTER: The vowel E is formed by approaching the lower jaw to the upper: A, E.

MONSIEUR JOURDAIN: A, E; A, E. By my troth, yes. Ah, how fine that is!

PHILOSOPHY-MASTER: And the vowel I, by bringing the jaws still nearer each other and stretching the two corners of the mouth towards the ears: A, E, I.

MONSIEUR JOURDAIN: A, E, I. I. I. I, I. That's true. Long live science!

PHILOSOPHY-MASTER: The vowel O is formed by opening the jaws and drawing together the two corners of the lips, upper and lower: O.

MONSIEUR JOURDAIN: O, O. There's nothing truer. A, E, I, O, I, O. That's admirable! I, O, I, O.

PHILOSOPHY-MASTER: The opening of the mouth happens to make a little circle which represents an O.

MONSIEUR JOURDAIN: O, O, O. You are right! O. Ah, what a fine thing it is to know something!

PHILOSOPHY-MASTER: The vowel U is formed by bringing the teeth near together without completely joining them, and thrusting the two lips outward, also bringing them near together without completely joining them: U.

MONSIEUR JOURDAIN: U, U. There's nothing truer. U.

PHILOSOPHY-MASTER: Your two lips thrust out as if you were making a face, whence it results that if you want to make a face at someone and jest at him, you have only to say to him "U."

MONSIEUR JOURDAIN: U, U. That's true. Ah, why did I not study sooner to know all that!

PHILOSOPHY-MASTER: Tomorrow we shall look at the other letters, which are the consonants.

MONSIEUR JOURDAIN: Are there strange things about them as about these?

PHILOSOPHY-MASTER: Without a doubt. The consonant D, for example, is pronounced by clapping the tongue above above the upper teeth: DE.

MONSIEUR JOURDAIN: DE, DE, Yes. Oh, what charming, charming things!

PHILOSOPHY-MASTER: The F, by pressing the upper teeth against the lower lip: EF.

MONSIEUR JOURDAIN: EF, EF. That's the truth. Oh, my father and my mother, how I hold a grudge against you!

PHILOSOPHY-MASTER: And the R, by carrying the tip of the tongue to the top of the palate, so that being grazed by the air that comes out with force, it yields to it and comes back always to the same place, making a kind of trill: R. AR.

MONSIEUR JOURDAIN: R, AR, AR. R, AR, AR, AR. That's true. Oh, what a clever man you are! And how I have lost time! R, AR, AR.

PHILOSOPHY-MASTER: I'll explain all these strange things thoroughly to you.

MONSIEUR JOURDAIN: Pray do. But now, I must confide in you. I'm in love with a lady of great quality, and I could wish that you would help me write something to her in a little note that I will let fall at her feet.

PHILOSOPHY-MASTER: Very well.

MONSIEUR JOURDAIN: That will be gallant, yes?

PHILOSOPHY-MASTER: Doubtless. Is it verse that you wish to write her?

MONSIEUR JOURDAIN: No, no. I'll have no verse.

PHILOSOPHY-MASTER: Would you have only prose?

MONSIEUR JOURDAIN: No, I do not want either prose or verse.

PHILOSOPHY-MASTER: It must be one or the other.

MONSIEUR JOURDAIN: Why?

PHILOSOPHY-MASTER: Because, sir, there's only prose or verse to express ourselves.

MONSIEUR JOURDAIN: Only prose or verse?

PHILOSOPHY-MASTER: No, sir, everything that is not prose is verse; everything that is not verse is prose.

MONSIEUR JOURDAIN: And when we talk, what may that be, then?

PHILOSOPHY-MASTER: Prose.

MONSIEUR JOURDAIN: Well! When I say, "Nicole, bring me my slippers, and give me my nightcap," that's prose?

PHILOSOPHY-MASTER: Yes, sir.

MONSIEUR JOURDAIN: By my troth! For more than forty years I have been speaking prose without knowing anything about it! And I am very obliged to you for having taught me that. Well then, I would like to put into a note to her: "Beautiful marchioness, your lovely eyes make me die of love," but I want that put in a gallant manner and be nicely turned.

PHILOSOPHY-MASTER: Put it that the fires of her eyes reduce your heart to cinders; that you suffer night and day for her the torments of a . . .

MONSIEUR JOURDAIN: No, no, no. I want none of that; I only want you to say "Beautiful marchioness, your lovely eyes make me die of love."

PHILOSOPHY-MASTER: You will have to lengthen the thing a little.

MONSIEUR JOURDAIN: No, no, I say, I only want those words I said in the note, but turned stylishly, well arranged, neatly. Pray tell me, just to see, the diverse ways they could be put.

PHILOSOPHY-MASTER: We could place them first of all as you said: "Beautiful marchioness, your lovely eyes make me die of love." Or else: "Of love to die make, beautiful marchioness, me, your beautiful eyes." Or perhaps: "Your lovely eyes, of love make me, beautiful marchioness, die." Or perhaps: "Die, your lovely eyes, beautiful marchioness, of love make me." Or else: "Me make your lovely eyes die, beautiful marchioness, of love."

MONSIEUR JOURDAIN: But, of all those ways, which is the best?

PHILOSOPHY-MASTER: The way you said it: "Beautiful marchioness, your lovely eyes make me die of love."

MONSIEUR JOURDAIN: Yet I never studied, and I make the whole thing at the first try! I thank you with all my heart, and I pray you to come tomorrow early.

PHILOSOPHY-MASTER: I shall not fail to do so. *(He goes out)*.

MONSIEUR JOURDAIN: *(To his Lackey)*. What? Are my clothes not come yet?

THE LACKEY: No, sir.

MONSIEUR JOURDAIN: That cursed tailor keeps me waiting when I have so much to do! I'm wild with anger. May the quartan fever shake that tormentor of a tailor! To the devil with the tailor! May the plague choke the tailor! If I had him here now, that detestable tailor, that dog of a tailor, that traitor of a tailor, I'd . . .

(Enter, the Tailor).

SCENE V

(The Tailor, entering, is followed by his assistants, carrying a suit of clothes for Monsieur Jourdain).

MONSIEUR JOURDAIN: Oh, you're here? I was getting into a rage against you.

MASTER-TAILOR: I was not able to come sooner, and I put twenty fellows to work at your clothes.

MONSIEUR JOURDAIN: You have sent me some silk hose so narrow that I had all the difficulty in the world putting them on, and already there are two broken stitches.

MASTER-TAILOR: They become bigger, too much so.

MONSIEUR JOURDAIN: Yes, if I always burst the stitches. You have also had made for me a pair of shoes that pinch furiously.

MASTER-TAILOR: Not at all, sir.

MONSIEUR JOURDAIN: How, not at all!

MASTER-TAILOR: No, they don't pinch you at all.

MONSIEUR JOURDAIN: I tell you, they pinch me.

MASTER-TAILOR: You imagine that.

MONSIEUR JOURDAIN: I imagine it because I feel it. That's a good reason for you!

MASTER-TAILOR: Stay, here is the finest court-costume, and the best matched. It's a masterpiece to have invented a serious costume that is not black. And I give six trials to the best tailors to equal it.

MONSIEUR JOURDAIN: What the devil is this? You have turned the flowers upside down.

MASTER-TAILOR: You did not tell me, did you, that you wanted them right side up?

MONSIEUR JOURDAIN: Did I have to tell you that?

MASTER-TAILOR: Yes, truly. All the people of quality wear them that way.

MONSIEUR JOURDAIN: The people of quality wear the flowers upside down?

MASTER-TAILOR: Yes, sir.

MONSIEUR JOURDAIN: Oh! 'Tis very well, then.

MASTER-TAILOR: If you like, I'll put them right side up.

MONSIEUR JOURDAIN: No, no.

MASTER-TAILOR: You need only to say the word.

MONSIEUR JOURDAIN: No, I tell you. You've made it very well. Do you think the suit is going to look well on me?

MASTER-TAILOR: A fine question! I defy a painter with his brush to do anything that would fit you better. I have a fellow in my place who is the greatest genius in the world at mounting a rhinegrave, and another who, for concocting a doublet, is the hero of the age.

MONSIEUR JOURDAIN: The perruque and the plumes: are they as they should be?

MASTER-TAILOR: Everything's well.

MONSIEUR JOURDAIN: *(Looking at the tailor's clothes).* Oh, Oh! Mr. Tailor, here's my stuff from the last suit you made for me. I know it well.

MASTER-TAILOR: You see, the stuff seemed so fine that I had a mind to cut a suit for myself out of it.

MONSIEUR JOURDAIN: Yes, but you should not have slashed it out of mine.

MASTER-TAILOR: Will you put on your costume?

MONSIEUR JOURDAIN: Yes, give it to me.

MASTER-TAILOR: Stay. The matter goes not so. I have brought men to dress you in set rhythm; these kinds of suits are put on with ceremony. Ho, there! Come in, you!

Put this suit on the gentleman the way you do with people of quality.

(Four apprentice-tailors enter, two of whom pull off Monsieur Jourdain's straight breeches made for his morning exercises, and two others pull off his waistcoat; then they put on him his new clothes, to music; while Monsieur Jourdain struts among them and shows them his clothes to see if he is well dressed. All this to the accompaniment of instrumental music.)

APPRENTICE-TAILOR: My dear gentleman, please to give the apprentices some small gratuity.

MONSIEUR JOURDAIN: What did you call me?

APPRENTICE-TAILOR: My dear gentleman.

MONSIEUR JOURDAIN: My dear gentleman! That's what it is to dress like people of quality! Go all your life dressed like a shopkeeper and they'll never call you "My dear gentleman." Here, take this for the "My dear gentleman."

APPRENTICE-TAILOR: My Lord, we are very much obliged to you.

MONSIEUR JOURDAIN: "My Lord!" Ha, ha, ha! "My Lord!" Wait, friend. "My Lord" deserves something, and it's not a little word, that "My Lord." Take this. That's what "My Lord" gives you.

APPRENTICE-TAILOR: My Lord, we will drink to the health of Your Grace.

MONSIEUR JOURDAIN: "Your Grace!" Ha, ha, ha! Wait, you're not to go. To me, "Your Grace!" By my troth, if he goes as far as "Highness," he will have all my purse. Stay. That's for my "Grace."

APPRENTICE-TAILOR: My Lord, we thank you very humbly for your liberality.

MONSIEUR JOURDAIN: He did well, I was going to give him everything.

(The four apprentice-tailors regale themselves with a dance, which comprises the Second Interlude.)

ACT THREE

SCENE I *(M. Jourdain and Lackeys)*

MONSIEUR JOURDAIN: Follow me, that I may go to make some show of my clothes in the town. And above all things, be careful, both of you, to walk close at my heels, so that it may be clearly seen that you belong to me.

LACKEYS: Yes, sir.

MONSIEUR JOURDAIN: Call Nicole for me, that I may give her some orders. Don't move, there she is.

SCENE II

(Nicole, M. Jourdain, Lackeys)

MONSIEUR JOURDAIN: Nicole!

NICOLE: Yes, sir?

MONSIEUR JOURDAIN: Listen.

NICOLE: *(Giggling uncontrollably)* . . . He, he, he, he, he!

MONSIEUR JOURDAIN: What are you laughing about?

NICOLE: He, he, he, he, he, he!

MONSIEUR JOURDAIN: What does the jade mean by this?

NICOLE: He, he, he! Oh, how you are got up! He, he, he!

MONSIEUR JOURDAIN: What's that?

NICOLE: Oh, Oh! Lordy! He, he, he, he, he!

MONSIEUR JOURDAIN: What kind of saucy baggage is this? Are you mocking me?

NICOLE: Indeed no, sir, I should be very sorry to do so. He, he, he, he, he!

MONSIEUR JOURDAIN: I'll give you a slap if you go on laughing.

NICOLE: Sir, I can't help it. He, he, he, he, he, he!

MONSIEUR JOURDAIN: Are you not going to stop?

NICOLE: Sir, I beg pardon. But you are so comical that I couldn't keep from laughing. He, he, he!

MONSIEUR JOURDAIN: Why, what insolence!

NICOLE: You're absolutely comical like that. He, he!

MONSIEUR JOURDAIN: I'm going to . . .

NICOLE: Pray excuse me. He, he, he, he!

MONSIEUR JOURDAIN: Listen. If you go on laughing the least bit, I swear I'll give ye the biggest box on the ears ever given.

NICOLE: Well, sir, it's done, I'll laugh no more.

MONSIEUR JOURDAIN: Take good care not to. By and by you must clean . . .

NICOLE: He, he!

MONSIEUR JOURDAIN: That you clean nicely . . .

NICOLE: He, he!

MONSIEUR JOURDAIN: You must, I say, clean the drawingroom and . . .

NICOLE: He, he!

MONSIEUR JOURDAIN: Again?

NICOLE: *(Tumbling down with laughter).* Hold, sir, beat me rather, and let me laugh my fill, it'll do me more good. He, he, he, he!

MONSIEUR JOURDAIN: I'm wild.

NICOLE: Have mercy, sir! Pray let me laugh. He, he, he!

MONSIEUR JOURDAIN: If I catch you . . .

NICOLE: Si-ir! I shall burst . . . Ay! if I don't laugh. He, he, he!

MONSIEUR JOURDAIN: But did anyone ever see such a hussy as that, who comes to laugh in my face instead of taking my orders?

NICOLE: What would you have me do, sir?

MONSIEUR JOURDAIN: Why, you jade, that you remember to make my house ready for the company that's coming by and by.

NICOLE: Oh, faith, I don't feel like laughing more. And all your companies who make such a disorder here that the word is enough to put me in a bad humor.

MONSIEUR JOURDAIN: Why, should I shut my house door to everyone for your sake?

NICOLE: You should at least shut it to some people.

SCENE III

(Madame Jourdain, Monsieur Jourdain, Nicole, Two Lackeys)

MADAME JOURDAIN: Ah, ah! Here's another to-do! What's this, what's this, husband, this outfit you have on there?

Don't you care a fig what people think of you to get yourself harnessed up like that? And do you want yourself laughed at everywhere?

MONSIEUR JOURDAIN: None but fools and blockheads, wife, will laugh at me.

MADAME JOURDAIN: Truly, they've not waited till now, and it's a long time now that your ways have provided a laugh for all the world.

MONSIEUR JOURDAIN: Who's all the world, pray?

MADAME JOURDAIN: All that world is a world of people who are right and who are wiser than you. For my part, I am scandalized at the life you lead. I don't recognize our house any more. One would say 'tis the beginning of carnival here, every day; and from break of day, for fear it might lack, there's nothing to be heard here but a hullabaloo of fiddles and singers which disturbs the whole neighborhood.

NICOLE: Madame speaks well. I'll never be able to get my housekeeping done properly with that set of folk you have come here. They have feet that hunt for mud in every corner of the town to bring it here; and poor Françoise almost has her face to the floor, scrubbing the boards that your fine masters come to dirty up every day, regularly.

MONSIEUR JOURDAIN: My word, our serving-maid Nicole! You have a nimbly wagging tongue for a peasant.

MADAME JOURDAIN: Nicole is right, and she has more

sense than you have. I'd like to know what you expect to do with a dancing-master, at your age?

NICOLE: And with a hulking fencing-master who comes stamping his feet, shaking the whole house and tearing up all the flooring in our drawing-room.

MONSIEUR JOURDAIN: Be quiet, both of you, servant and wife!

MADAME JOURDAIN: And you're learning to dance for when you'll have no legs to dance on?

NICOLE: Do you want to murder someone?

MONSIEUR JOURDAIN: Peace, I say! You are ignorant women, both of you, and you don't know the advantages of all this.

MADAME JOURDAIN: You should be thinking, rather, of marrying off your daughter, who is of an age to be provided with a husband.

MONSIEUR JOURDAIN: I'll think of marrying off my daughter when a suitable match comes along. But I also want to learn the fine things.

NICOLE: And I heard say, Madame, that today he took a master of philosophy, to thicken the soup!

MONSIER JOURDAIN: Very well. I've a mind to have wit and to reason about things with civil people.

MADAME JOURDAIN: Don't you intend, one of these days, to go to school and, at your age, to have yourself whipped?

MONSIEUR JOURDAIN: Why not? Would to God I were

whipped this minute in front of everyone, but that I knew what they learn at school!

NICOLE: Yes, faith, that would put you into better shape!

MONSIEUR JOURDAIN: No doubt.

MADAME JOURDAIN: All this is very important to the management of your house.

MONSIEUR JOURDAIN: Assuredly. You talk, both of you, like brute beasts, and I'm ashamed of your ignorance. I'm asking you: what are these words you are speaking here? Do you know?

MADAME JOURDAIN: Yes, I know that what I'm saying is well said and that you ought to be thinking of living in another way.

MONSIEUR JOURDAIN: I'm not talking about that, I tell you. I'm asking: do you know what the words are that you are saying here?

MADAME JOURDAIN: They are words that are very sensible—and your conduct is by no means so.

MONSIEUR JOURDAIN: I'm not speaking of that, I tell you. I'm asking: what is it that I'm now speaking to you this minute, what is it?

MADAME JOURDAIN: Stuff and nonsense.

MONSIEUR JOURDAIN: No, no, that's not it. What is it we are both saying, what language is it that we are now speaking?

MADAME JOURDAIN: Well?

MONSIEUR JOURDAIN: How is it called?

MADAME JOURDAIN: It's called whatever you want to call it.

MONSIEUR JOURDAIN: 'Tis prose, you ignorant creature.

MADAME JOURDAIN: Prose?

MONSIEUR JOURDAIN: Yes, prose. Everything is prose that is not verse; and everything that's not verse is prose. Now then! See what it is to study! And you *(to Nicole)*, do you know very well how you must do to say U?

NICOLE: How?

MONSIEUR JOURDAIN: Just say U, to see.

NICOLE: Oh well: U.

MONSIEUR JOURDAIN: What is it that you do?

NICOLE: I say U.

MONSIEUR JOURDAIN: Yes, but, when you say U, what do you do?

NICOLE: I do what you tell me to.

MONSIEUR JOURDAIN: Oh, how strange it is to have to deal with idiots! You thrust your lips out and bring your lower jaw to your upper jaw: U. Do you see? I make a pout: U.

NICOLE: Yes, that's beautiful.

MADAME JOURDAIN: Now isn't that admirable!

MONSIEUR JOURDAIN: But 'tis quite another thing, if you have seen O, and DE, DE, and EF, EF.

MADAME JOURDAIN: What's all this rigmarole, for heaven's sake?

NICOLE: What does all this cure us of?

MONSIEUR JOURDAIN: It makes me wild when I see these ignorant women.

MADAME JOURDAIN: Go, go, you ought to send all those people packing with their stuff and nonsense.

NICOLE: And above all, that great gawk of a fencing master, who fills my house with dust.

MONSIEUR JOURDAIN: How now! This fencing master seems to stick in your gizzard. I'll soon let you see your impertinence. *(He has the foils brought and hands one to Nicole)*. There. Demonstrative reason. The line of the body. And when they push in carte you need only do so. And when they push in tierce, you need only do so. This is the way never to be killed. And is it not fine to be assured of one's action, when fighting against someone? There, push me a little, to see.

NICOLE: Well then, what? *(Nicole pushes, giving him several thrusts)*.

MONSIEUR JOURDAIN: Gently, hold there! Oh, gently! The devil take the hussy!

NICOLE: You bade me push.

MONSIEUR JOURDAIN: Yes. But you pushed tierce, before you pushed carte, and you had no patience to let me parry.

MADAME JOURDAIN: You are a fool, husband, with all your fantasies, and this has come to you since you took it into your head to haunt the nobility.

MONSIEUR JOURDAIN: When I haunt the nobility, I show

my judgment: and that's finer than to haunt your shop-keepers.

MADAME JOURDAIN: Oh yes, truly! There's a great deal to get by consorting with your nobles, and you operated well with your fine Count you were so taken with!

MONSIEUR JOURDAIN: Peace! Think what you're saying. You very well know, wife, that you don't know whom you're talking about, when you talk about him! He's a person of more importance than you think: a great Lord, respected at court, and who talks to the King just as I'm talking to you. Is it not a thing which does me honor completely, that a person of that quality is seen to come so often to my house and who calls me his dear friend, treating me as if I were his equal? He has more kindness for me that one would ever imagine; and, in front of everyone, he shows so much affection for me that I myself am embarrassed.

MADAME JOURDAIN: Yes, he has a kindness for you, and shows his affection, but he borrows your money.

MONSIEUR JOURDAIN: Well! Is it not an honor for me to lend money to a man of that condition? And can I do less for a lord who calls me his dear friend?

MADAME JOURDAIN: And this lord, what does he do for you?

MONSIEUR JOURDAIN: Things that would astonish you if you knew them.

MADAME JOURDAIN: Well, what?

MONSIEUR JOURDAIN: Basta! I cannot explain myself.

'Tis enough that if I have lent him money, he'll pay it back well, and that before long.

MADAME JOURDAIN: Yes. You expect that.

MONSIEUR JOURDAIN: Assuredly. Did he not say so?

MADAME JOURDAIN: Yes, yes, he'll not fail to fail to do so.

MONSIEUR JOURDAIN: He swore it on the faith of a gentleman.

MADAME JOURDAIN: Stuff and nonsense!

MONSIEUR JOURDAIN: Oh, oh! You are mighty obstinate, wife. I tell you he'll keep his word, I'm sure of it.

MADAME JOURDAIN: And I—I'm sure he will not, and that all his show of affection is only to flatter you.

MONSIEUR JOURDAIN: Hold your tongue. Here he is.

MADAME JOURDAIN: That's all we needed! He's come again perhaps to borrow something from you. The very sight of him cuts my appetite.

MONSIEUR JOURDAIN: I tell you, hold your tongue.

SCENE IV

Enter the Count Dorante

DORANTE: My dear friend, Monsieur Jourdain, how do you do?

MONSIEUR JOURDAIN: Very well, sir, to render you my small services.

DORANTE: And Madame Jourdain whom I see there, how is she?

MADAME JOURDAIN: Madame Jourdain is as well as she can be.

DORANTE: How now! Monsieur Jourdain, you are superbly well dressed!

MONSIEUR JOURDAIN: You see.

DORANTE: You have an absolutely fine air in that suit, and we have no young fellows at court who are better built than you.

MONSIEUR JOURDAIN: He, he!

MADAME JOURDAIN: *(Aside)* He scratches him where it itches.

DORANTE: Turn around. 'Tis absolutely elegant.

MADAME JOURDAIN: *(Aside)* Yes, as big a fool behind as in front.

DORANTE: Faith, Monsieur Jourdain, I was strangely impatient to see you. You are the man in the world I esteem most, and I was talking about you again this morning at the King's levee.

MONSIEUR JOURDAIN: You honor me greatly, sir. *(To Madame Jourdain)* At the King's levee!

DORANTE: Come, put on . . .[1]

MONSIEUR JOURDAIN: Sir, I know the respect I owe you.

DORANTE: Heavens! Be covered; pray, no ceremony between us.

---

[1] *The reference is to M. Jourdain's hat, which he has removed.*

MONSIEUR JOURDAIN: Sir . . .

DORANTE: Put it on, I tell you, Monsieur Jourdain; you are my friend.

MONSIEUR JOURDAIN: Sir, I am your humble servant.

DORANTE: I won't be covered if you won't.

MONSIEUR JOURDAIN: *(Puts on his hat).* I prefer to be uncivil rather than troublesome.

DORANTE: I am in your debt, as you know.

MADAME JOURDAIN: *(Aside).* Yes, we know it all too well.

DORANTE: You have generously lent me money upon several occasions, and you have obliged me with the best grace in the world, assuredly.

MONSIEUR JOURDAIN: Sir, you are jesting at me.

DORANTE: But I know how to repay what is lent me, and to acknowledge the gratifications rendered me.

MONSIEUR JOURDAIN: I have no doubt of it, sir.

DORANTE: I want to pull out of this business with you, and I came here to make up our accounts together.

MONSIEUR JOURDAIN: *(Aside to Madame Jourdain).* Well, now! You see your impertinence, wife!

DORANTE: I am a man who likes to repay debts as quickly as possible.

MONSIUR JOURDAIN: *(Aside to Madame Jourdain).* I told you so.

DORANTE: Let's see what 'tis I owe you.

MONSIEUR JOURDAIN: *(Aside to Madame Jourdain).* There you are, with your ridiculous suspicions.

DORANTE: Do you well remember all the money you have lent me?

MONSIEUR JOURDAIN: I believe so. I made a little note of it. Here it is. At one time you were given two hundred *louis d'or.*

DORANTE: That's true.

MONSIEUR JOURDAIN: Another time, six-score.

DORANTE: Yes.

MONSIEUR JOURDAIN: And another time, a hundred and forty.

DORANTE: You're right.

MONSIEUR JOURDAIN: These three items make four hundred and sixty *louis d'or,* which comes to five thousand and sixty *livres.*

DORANTE: The account is quite right. Five thousand and sixty *livres.*

MONSIEUR JOURDAIN: One thousand eight hundred and thirty-two *livres* to your plume-maker.

DORANTE: Exactly.

MONSIEUR JOURDAIN: Two thousand seven hundred and four-score *livres* to your tailor.

DORANTE: That's true.

MONSIEUR JOURDAIN: Four thousand three hundred and seventy-nine *livres,* twelve *sols* and eight *deniers* to your tradesman.

DORANTE: Quite right. Twelve *sols,* eight *deniers.* The account is exact.

MONSIEUR JOURDAIN: And a thousand seven hundred and forty-eight *livres,* seven *sols,* four *deniers,* to your saddler.

DORANTE: All that is right enough. What does that come to?

MONSIEUR JOURDAIN: Sum total, fifteen thousand eight hundred *livres.*

DORANTE: The sum total is exact: fifteen thousand eight hundred *livres.* To which add two hundred *pistoles* that you are going to lend me, that will make exactly eighteen thousand francs, which I shall pay you at the first opportunity.

MADAME JOURDAIN: *(Aside to M. Jourdain).* Well, didn't I guess it?

MONSIEUR JOURDAIN: *(Aside to Mme. Jourdain).* Peace!

DORANTE: Will that incommode you, to lend me the amount I say?

MONSIEUR JOURDAIN: Oh, no!

MADAME JOURDAIN: *(Aside to M. Jourdain).* That man is making a milch-cow out of you!

MONSIEUR JOURDAIN: *(Aside to Mme. Jourdain).* Hold your tongue!

DORANTE: If that incommodes you, I will seek it elsewhere.

MONSIEUR JOURDAIN: No, sir.

MADAME JOURDAIN: *(Aside to M. Jourdain).* He'll not be satisfied till he has ruined you.

MONSIEUR JOURDAIN: *(Aside to Mme. Jourdain).* Hold your tongue, I say!

DORANTE: You have only to tell me if that inconveniences you.

MONSIEUR JOURDAIN: Not at all, sir.

MADAME JOURDAIN: *(Aside to M. Jourdain).* He's a veritable wheedler!

MONSIEUR JOURDAIN: *(Aside to Mme. Jourdain).* Will you hold your tongue!

MADAME JOURDAINS *(Aside to M. Jourdain).* He'll drain you to the last penny.

MONSIEUR JOURDAIN: *(Aside to Mme. Jourdain).* Will you be quiet?

DORANTE: I have a great many people who would gladly lend it to me; but since you are my best friend, I thought I should be doing you a wrong if I asked someone else for it.

MONSIEUR JOURDAIN: It's too much of an honor, sir, that you do me. I'll go, to fetch your thingumajig.

MADAME JOURDAIN: *(Aside to M. Jourdain).* What! You're going still further to lend him that?

MONSIEUR JOURDAIN: *(Aside to Mme. Jourdain).* What can I do? Would you have me refuse a man of this rank, who spoke about me this morning at the King's levee?

MADAME JOURDAIN: *(Aside to M. Jourdain).* Go, you are a veritable dupe.

SCENE V

(Dorante, Mme. Jourdain, Nicole)

DORANTE: You appear to be very melancholy. What ails you, Madame Jourdain?

MADAME JOURDAIN: I have a head bigger than my fist, even if it's not swollen.

DORANTE: Where is Mademoiselle your daughter, that I don't see her?

MADAME JOURDAIN: Mademoiselle my daughter is right where she is.

DORANTE: How goes she?

MADAME JOURDAIN: She goes on her two legs.

DORANTE: Would you not like, one of these days, to come with her to see the ballet and the comedy they are acting at court?

MADAME JOURDAIN: Yes, truly, we've a strong inclination to laugh, a great inclination to laugh, have we.

DORANTE: I imagine, Madame Jourdain, that you must have had a great many admirers in your youth, beautiful and of a pleasant humor as you were.

MADAME JOURDAIN: By Our Lady, sir, is it that Madame

Jourdain is decrepit, and does her head already shake with the palsy?

DORANTE: Oh! My word, Madame Jourdain, I beg pardon. I did not remember that you are young, and my mind is often distracted. Pray excuse my impertinence.

SCENE VI

(Monsieur Jourdain, Madame Jourdain, Dorante, Nicole)

MONSIEUR JOURDAIN: Here are a good two hundred *louis d'or*.

DORANTE: I assure you, Monsieur Jourdain, that I am absolutely yours, and that I am eager to render you a service at court.

MONSIEUR JOURDAIN: I'm altogether obliged to you.

DORANTE: If Madame Jourdain desires to see the royal entertainments, I will have the best places in the ballroom given to her.

MADAME JOURDAIN: Madame Jourdain kisses your hands.[1]

DORANTE: *(Aside to M. Jourdain)*. Our pretty marchioness, as I sent word to you in my note, will come here by and by for the ballet and the collation; I finally brought her to consent to the entertainment you wish to give her.

---

[1] *In effect, a phrase of refusal.*

MONSIEUR JOURDAIN: Let us withdraw a little farther off, for a certain reason.

DORANTE: 'Tis a week since I saw you, and I have not sent word to you regarding the diamond you put into my hands to make her a present for you. But it's because I had the greatest difficulty in conquering her scruples, and it's only today that she resolved to accept it.

MONSIEUR JOURDAIN: What was her opinion of it?

DORANTE: Marvellous. And I am very deceived if the beauty of that diamond does not have an admirable effect for you upon her.

MONSIEUR JOURDAIN: May Heaven grant it!

MADAME JOURDAIN: *(to Nicole).* Once he's with him he cannot leave him.

DORANTE: I made her value as she should the richness of that present and the grandeur of your love.

MONSIEUR JOURDAIN: These, sir, are kindnesses which overwhelm me; and I am in the very greatest confusion at seeing a person of your quality demean himself on my account as you do.

DORANTE: Are you jesting? Among friends, does one stop at these kinds of scruples? And would you not do the same thing for me, if the occasion offered?

MONSIEUR JOURDAIN: Oh, certainly, and with all my heart.

MADAME JOURDAIN: *(To Nicole).* His presence weighs me down!

DORANTE: As for me, I never mind anything when a friend must be served; and when you confessed to me the ardent passion you have formed for that delightful marchioness with whom I have contacts, you saw that I at once offered, of my own accord, to aid your passion.

MONSIEUR JOURDAIN: 'Tis true, these kindnesses are what confound me.

MADAME JOURDAIN: *(To Nicole)*. Will he never be gone?

NICOLE: They enjoy being together.

DORANTE: You took the right line to touch her heart. Women above all like the expenses we go to for them; and your frequent serenades, and your continual bouquets, that superb fireworks she beheld over the water, the diamond she has received from you, and the entertainment you are preparing for her, all this speaks much better in favor of your passion than all the words you might have spoken yourself.

MONSIEUR JOURDAIN: There are no expenditures I would not make if by that means I might find the road to her heart. A woman of quality has ravishing charms for me and it's an honor I would purchase at any price.

MADAME JOURDAIN: What can they talk so much about together? *(To Nicole)*. Go softly and listen a little.

DORANTE: By and by you will enjoy at your ease the pleasure of seeing her, and your eyes will have plenty of time to be satisfied.

MONSIEUR JOURDAIN: To be in full freedom, I have

arranged that my wife will go to dine with her sister, where she'll spend all the after-dinner time.

DORANTE: You have done prudently, for your wife might have embarrassed us. I have given for you the necessary order to the cook, and for all the things necessary for the ballet. 'Tis of my own invention and, provided the execution corresponds to the idea, I am sure it will be found . . .

MONSIEUR JOURDAIN: *(Sees that Nicole is listening, and gives her a slap).* Ho there! You're very impertinent! *(To Dorante).* Let us go, if you please.

SCENE VII

(Madame Jourdain, Nicole)

NICOLE: Upon my word, Madame, my curiosity has cost me something; but I believe there's a snake in the grass, for they were talking of some affair at which they did not want you to be.

MADAME JOURDAIN: Today's not the first time I've held suspicions of my husband, Nicole. I'm the most betrayed woman in the world, or there's some amour abroad. But let us think about my daughter. You know the love Cléonte has for her. He's a man I like, and I want to further his courtship and give him Lucile, if I can.

NICOLE: Forsooth, Madame, I'm the most delighted creature in the world at finding you entertain these feelings, since, if it's the master that hits your fancy, the valet hits mine no less, and I could wish our marriage could be concluded under the protection of theirs.

MADAME JOURDAIN: Go speak to him about it for me, and tell him to come to me presently that we may together make the demand to my husband for my daughter in marriage.

NICOLE: I fly at once to him, with joy, for I could not receive a pleasanter commission. *(Alone)*. I shall, I think, much gladden the two young people.

SCENE VIII

(Cléonte, Covielle, Nicole)

NICOLE: Ah! There you are, most fortunately. I'm an ambassadress of joy, and I come . . .

CLÉONTE: Begone, perfidious one, and do not come to amuse me with your treacherous words.

NICOLE: Is it thus you receive me . . .

CLÉONTE: Begone, I tell you, and go directly to your false mistress, tell her that never again in her life shall she deceive the too trusting Cléonte.

NICOLE: What fantasy is this? My dear Covielle, tell me a little what this means.

COVIELLE: Your dear Covielle, little hussy? Away,

quickly, get out of my sight, you jade, and leave me in peace.

NICOLE: What! You, too, come to . . .

COVIELLE: Out of my sight, I tell you, and don't speak to me again in your life.

NICOLE: Alack-a-day! What fly has bitten those two? Come, I must go recount this affair to my mistress.

SCENE IX

(Cléonte, Covielle)

CLÉONTE: What! Treat a lover in this way? And a lover who is the most faithful and passionate of lovers?

COVIELLE: It is a frightful thing that they have done to us both.

CLÉONTE: I display towards a woman all the ardor and tenderness that can be imagined; I love nothing in the world but her, and have nothing in my thoughts but her; she is all my care, all my desire, all my joy. I talk of naught but her, I think of naught but her, I have no dreams but of her, I breathe only because of her, my heart lives wholly in her; and see how so much love is worthily recompensed! I have been two days without seeing her, two days that are for me two horrible centuries. I meet her by chance. My heart, at that sight, is completely transported, my joy sparkles in my face; I fly with ecstasy towards her — and the faithless one averts her eyes and hurries past as if she had never seen me in her life!

COVIELLE: I say the same things as you.

CLÉONTE: Covielle, can one see the equal, ever, of this perfidy of the ungrateful Lucile?

COVIELLE: Or the perfidy, sir, of the villainous hussy, Nicole?

CLÉONTE: After so many ardent sacrifices, sighs, and vows that I have made to her charms!

COVIELLE: After so many assiduous tokens of esteem, cares and services that I rendered her in the kitchen!

CLÉONTE: So many tears I have shed at her knees!

COVIELLE: So many buckets of water I have drawn from the well for her!

CLÉONTE: So much warmth I have shown her in loving her more than myself!

COVIELLE: So much warmth I have endured in turning the spit for her!

CLÉONTE: She flees me with disdain!

COVIELLE: She turns her back on me brazenly!

CLÉONTE: It is perfidy worthy of the greatest punishments.

COVIELLE: It is treachery that merits a thousand slaps.

CLÉONTE: Pray don't ever get it into your head to plead her cause.

COVIELLE: I, sir? God forbid!

CLÉONTE: Never come to excuse the action of this faithless woman.

COVIELLE: Fear not.

CLÉONTE: No, for you see, all your speeches in her defence will be of no avail.

COVIELLE: Who's dreaming of that?

CLÉONTE: I want to conserve my resentment against her and want us to cease all contacts.

COVIELLE: I agree to't.

CLÉONTE: This Count who visits her perhaps pleases her eye; and her mind, I well see, lets itself be dazzled by quality. But I need, for my honor, forestall the scandal of her inconstancy. I want to take as many steps as she towards the change to which I see her swiftly going, and not leave her all the glory of casting me off.

COVIELLE: That's very well said, and I enter, for my part, into all your feelings.

CLÉONTE: Lend a hand to my chagrin and strengthen my resolution against all the remains of love that could plead for her. I conjure you, speak all the ill you can of her to me. Make for me a portrait of her that will render her despicable; and point up well, to disgust me, all the faults that you can see in her.

COVIELLE: A portrait of her, sir? Oh, there's a pretty stuck-up, well made piece of conceit for you to become so enamored of! I see nothing in her that is not very mediocre, and you will find a hundred women who will be more worthy of you. First of all, she has small eyes.

CLÉONTE: That's true, she has small eyes, but they are full of fire, they are the brightest, the keenest in the world, the most touching eyes that one may see.

COVIELLE: She has a large mouth.

CLÉONTE: Yes; but upon it one sees charms never seen on other mouths; and that mouth, the very sight of which arouses desires, is the most attractive, the most amorous in the world.

COVIELLE: As to her shape, she's not tall.

CLÉONTE: No! but she is graceful and well proportioned.

COVIELLE: She affects a negligence in her speech and in her actions.

CLÉONTE: That's true; but she is condoned all that, for her manners are so engaging, they have an indescribable charm, to penetrate our hearts.

COVIELLE: As to her wit . . .

CLÉONTE: Oh, that she has, Covielle, the finest, the most delicate!

COVIELLE: Her conversation . . .

CLÉONTE: Her conversation is delightful.

COVIELLE: She is always serious . . .

CLÉONTE: Would you have broad pleasantries, those always expansive gaieties? And do you see anything more impertinent than those women who laugh in season and out of season?

COVIELLE: But in short she is as capricious as any woman in the world.

CLÉONTE: Yes, she is capricious, I grant you; but everything becomes fair ladies well, one suffers everything from the fair sex.

COVIELLE: Since that's the way it goes, I clearly see that you wish to go on loving her.

CLÉONTE: For my part, I'd like better to die; and I am going to hate her as much as I have loved her.

COVIELLE: By what means, if you find her so perfect?

CLÉONTE: Therein shall my vengeance be more striking, therein I shall the better show the strength of my courage, by hating her, casting her off, though finding her most beautiful, most full of charm, most amiable. Here she is.

SCENE X

(Cléonte, Lucile, Covielle, Nicole)

NICOLE: For my part, I was completely shocked at it.

LUCILE: Nicole, it can only be what I told you. But there he is.

CLÉONTE: I don't even want to speak to her.

COVIELLE: I'll imitate you.

LUCILE: Why, what is it, Cléonte? What's the matter with you?

NICOLE: Why, what's the matter with you, Covielle?

LUCILE: What grief possesses you?

NICOLE: What bad humour grips you?

LUCILE: Are you dumb, Cléonte?

NICOLE: Have you lost your tongue, Covielle?

CLÉONTE: Is this not villainous!

COVIELLE: It's Judas!

LUCILE: I see clearly that our encounter of a short time ago has troubled your mind.

CLÉONTE: Oh ho! She sees what she has done.

NICOLE: Our [curt] greeting of this morning has got your goat.

COVIELLE: *(To Cléonte)*. She has guessed the difficulty.

LUCILE: Is it not true, Cléonte, that this is the cause of your spleen?

CLÉONTE: Yes, perfidious one, it is, since I must speak; and I have this to say: you shall not triumph in your faithlessness as you think you will, for I shall be the first to break with you, and you won't have the advantage of driving me away. No doubt I shall have trouble in conquering the love I have for you; 'twill cause me griefs. I will suffer for a while; but I shall manage it, and I would rather stab myself to death than have the weakness to return to you.

COVIELLE: Me, too.

LUCILE: What a furore over nothing. I want to tell you, Cléonte, the reason that made me avoid joining you this morning.

CLÉONTE: No, I do not want to hear anything . . .

NICOLE: I want to tell you the cause that made us pass so quickly.

COVIELLE: I don't want to hear a thing.

LUCILE: Know that this morning . . .

CLÉONTE: *(Continuing to walk, ignoring her).* No, I tell you.

NICOLE: *(Following Covielle).* Learn that . . .

COVIELLE: *(Continuing to walk, ignoring her).* No, traitress.

LUCILE: Listen.

CLÉONTE: Nothing doing.

NICOLE: Let me speak.

COVIELLE: I'm deaf.

LUCILE: Cléonte!

CLÉONTE: No.

NICOLE: Covielle!

COVIELLE: Not at all.

LUCILE: Stop!

CLÉONTE: Stuff and nonsense!

NICOLE: Listen to me.

COVIELLE: Nonsense.

LUCILE: One moment.

CLÉONTE: Emphatically, no.

NICOLE: A little patience!

COVIELLE: Fiddlesticks!

LUCILE: Two words.

CLÉONTE: No, they've been said.

NICOLE: One word.

COVIELLE: No more transactions.

LUCILE: *(Stopping).* Oh, well, since you don't want to listen to me, stick to your opinion and do what you like.

NICOLE: *(Stopping).* Since you act like that, take the whole thing as you like.

CLÉONTE: *(Turning towards Lucille).* Let's know the reason, then, of such a fine reception.

LUCILE: *(In her turn, walking off).* It does not please me now to tell it.

COVIELLE: *(Turning towards Nicole).* Let us know something of this affair.

NICOLE: *(Walking off).* Me, I no longer want to tell you.

CLÉONTE: *(Following Lucile).* Tell me . . .

LUCILE: *(Still walking, and ignoring Cléonte).* No, I don't want to say anything.

COVIELLE: *(Following Nicole).* Say—

NICOLE: No, I'll say nothing.

CLÉONTE: For pity's sake!

LUCILE: No, I say.

COVIELLE: Have charity!

NICOLE: Nothing doing.

CLÉONTE: I beseech you.

LUCILE: Leave me . . .

COVIELLE: I conjure you.

NICOLE: Get out!

CLÉONTE: Lucile!

LUCILE: No.

COVIELLE: Nicole!

NICOLE: Not at all.

CLÉONTE: In the name of the gods!

LUCILE: I do not want to.

COVIELLE: Talk to me.

NICOLE: Emphatically no!

CLÉONTE: Clear up my doubts.

LUCILE: No, I'll do none of that.

COVIELLE: Ease my mind!

NICOLE: No, it does not please me to.

CLÉONTE: Well, since you are so little concerned to pull me out of my pain and to justify yourself for the shameful treatment you gave to my passion, you are seeing me, ungrateful creature, for the last time, and I am going far from you to die of grief and love.

COVIELLE: *(Starts to follow Cléonte, going).* And I—I will follow his steps.

LUCILE: Cléonte!

NICOLE: Covielle!

CLÉONTE: *(Stopping).* Eh?

COVIELLE: I beg pardon?

LUCILE: Where are you going?

CLÉONTE: Where I told you.

COVIELLE: We are going to die.

LUCILE: You are going to die, Cléonte?

CLÉONTE: Yes, cruel one, since you wish it.

LUCILE: I? I wish you to die?

CLÉONTE: Yes, you wish it.

LUCILE: Who told you so?

CLÉONTE: Is it not wishing it when you do not wish to clear up my suspicions?

LUCILE: Is it my fault? And, if you had wished to listen to me, would I not have told you that the experience of which you complain was caused this morning by the presence of an old aunt who insists that the mere approach of a man dishonors a maid? An aunt who lectures us constantly on this subject, and represents to us that all men are as devils that we must flee?

NICOLE: There's the whole secret of the affair.

CLÉONTE: Are you not deceiving me, Lucile?

COVIELLE: *(To Nicole).* Are you not piling it on?

LUCILE: There's nothing more true.

NICOLE: It's the thing as it is.

COVIELLE: Are we going to surrender to this?

CLÉONTE: Oh, Lucile, how with a word from your lips you are able to appease the things in my heart, and how easily we let ourselves be persuaded by the persons we love!

COVIELLE: How easily wheedled we are by these plaguy animals!

SCENE XI

(Madame Jourdain, Cléonte, Lucile, Covielle, Nicole)

MADAME JOURDAIN: Sir, I am very pleased to see you, and you arrive at the right moment. My husband is coming, quickly take your time to ask for Lucile in marriage.

CLÉONTE: Oh, madame! How sweet to me is that word, how it flatters my desires! Could I receive an order more charming, a favor more precious?

(Enter: Monsieur Jourdain, etc.)

SCENE XII

(M. Jourdain, Mme. Jourdain, Cléonte, Lucile, Covielle, Nicole)

CLÉONTE: Sir, I did not want to employ anyone to make a certain demand of you which I have long meditated. It concerns me sufficiently for me to undertake it myself; and, without other circumlocution, I will say that the honor of being your son-in-law is a glorious favor that I beg you to grant me.

MONSIEUR JOURDAIN: Before giving you a reply, sir, pray tell me whether you are a gentleman.

CLÉONTE: Sir, most people do not much hesitate on this

question. They speak the word boldly, having no scruple to take this title, and the custom of today seems to authorize the theft. For my part, I confess, I have feelings on this matter which are more delicate. I find any imposture unworthy of an honest man, and consider there is cowardice in disguising what Heaven made us at birth, or adorning ourselves in the eyes of the world with a stolen title, with the desire to pass ourselves off for what we are not. I was born, undoubtedly, of parents who held honorable employment. I have had the honor of six years' service in the army, and I find myself sufficiently well off to maintain a tolerable rank in the world; but for all that I certainly do not want to give myself a name which others in my place might believe they could claim, and I will tell you frankly that I am no gentleman.

MONSIEUR JOURDAIN: Your hand, sir![1] My daughter is not for you.

CLÉONTE: What?

MONSIEUR JOURDAIN: You are no gentleman, you shan't have my daughter.

MADAME JOURDAIN: What do you mean to say with your "gentleman"? Are we ourselves of the line of St. Louis?

MONSIEUR JOURDAIN: Hold your tongue, wife, I see what you are getting at!

---

[1] *Inappropriately using the gentlemanly gesture of shaking hands to conclude an agreement.*

MADAME JOURDAIN: Are we either of us descended otherwise than from plain citizens?

MONSIEUR JOURDAIN: There's the word I was expecting!

MADAME JOURDAIN: And was not your father a tradesman as well as mine?

MONSIEUR JOURDAIN: Plague take the woman! She never fails to do this! If your father was a tradesman, so much the worse for him; but as for mine, the people who say that are misinformed. All that I have to say to you is, that I want to have a son-in-law who is a gentleman.

MADAME JOURDAIN: For your daughter a husband is needed who is suitable to her, and it's worth more to have a well to do and well made honest man than a gentleman who is a pauper and badly made.

NICOLE: That's true. We have a gentleman's son in our village who is the most ill-shapen and the greatest booby I ever saw.

MONSIEUR JOURDAIN: Hold your tongue, impertinent creature! You're always thrusting yourself into the conversation. I've sufficient means for my daughter, all I need is honor, and I want to make her a marchioness.

MADAME JOURDAIN: A marchioness!

MONSIEUR JOURDAIN: Yes, marchioness.

MADAME JOURDAIN: Alas! May God preserve me from it!

MONSIEUR JOURDAIN: It's a thing I've decided.

MADAME JOURDAIN: It's a thing I'll never consent to. Marriages above one's station are always subject to grievous inconveniences. I won't have a son-in-law who can reproach my daughter for her parents, I don't want her to have children who will be ashamed to call me their grandmother. Should she come to visit me in the equipage of a great lady and should she fail, by accident, to greet someone of the neighborhood, they'd not fail to say a hundred stupid things at once. "Do you see," they'd say, "this lady marchioness who gives herself such haughty airs? She's the daughter of Monsieur Jourdain, who was all too glad, when she was little, to play house with us; she's not always been so lofty as she now is; and her two grandfathers sold cloth near St. Innocent's Gate. They amassed a fortune for their children, they're paying dearly for it now, perhaps, in the other world, for people certainly don't get that rich by honest means." I won't have all that gossip, and I want, in short, a man who will be grateful to me for my daughter and to whom I can say, "Sit you down there, son-in-law, and have dinner with me."

MONSIEUR JOURDAIN: Surely those are the sentiments of a narrow mind, to want to remain always in a mean condition. Let me have no more replies: my daughter shall be a marchioness despite everyone. And, if you put me into a rage, I'll make a duchess of her.

MADAME JOURDAIN: Cléonte, don't lose courage yet. Follow me, my daughter, and come tell him resolutely that, if you don't have him, you'll marry no one.

SCENE XIII

(Cléonte, Covielle)

COVIELLE: You've made a fine piece of work, with your pretty sentiments.

CLÉONTE: What could you want? I have a scruple on that point that precedent cannot conquer.

COVIELLE: You make yourself ridiculous, don't you, in taking the matter seriously with a man like that? Don't you see he's a fool? And would it cost you anything to accommodate yourself to his chimeras?

CLÉONTE: You're right. But I did not believe that it was necessary to bring proofs of nobility in order to be son-in-law of Monsieur Jourdain.

COVIELLE: Ha, ha, ha!

CLÉONTE: What are you laughing at?

COVIELLE: At a thought I've just had to play our good-man a trick and help you obtain what you wish.

CLÉONTE: How?

COVIELLE: The idea is absolutely droll.

CLÉONTE: What is it?

COVIELLE: There was performed a little while ago a certain masquerade which comes in here as well as possible, and which I intend to insert in a farcical trick I want to play our coxcomb. All this smacks of the theatre, a little; but, with him, we may risk anything, there's no need to study finesse, and he is the man to play his part to a wonder in it, to fall for all the rigmaroles we care to tell him. I have the actors and the costumes ready, just let me be.

CLÉONTE: But inform me.

COVIELLE: I will instruct you in everything. Let us withdraw, there he is, returning.

SCENE XIV

(Monsieur Jourdain, Lackey)

MONSIEUR JOURDAIN: What the devil is this? They have nothing to reproach me with but the great lords; and for my part I see nothing so fine as to haunt the great lords; there's nothing but honor and civility with them, and I would it had cost me two fingers of a hand to have been born a count or a marquis.

LACKEY: Sir, here's the Count, and a lady he is leading in.

MONSIEUR JOURDAIN: Good Heavens, I've some order to give. Tell them I'll be back here presently.

SCENE XV

(Dorimène, Dorante, Lackey)

LACKEY: My master says . . . uh . . . that he'll be back here presently.

DORANTE: That's good.

DORIMÈNE: I don't know, Dorante; I'm still taking a strange step here by allowing myself to be brought by you to this house where I know nobody.

DORANTE: What place, then, Madame, would you wish my love should choose for your entertainment since, to avoid scandal, you allow neither your house nor mine?

DORIMÈNE: Why not mention that every day I am insensibly engaging myself to receive too great proofs of your passion? Try as I will to hold out against things, you wear down my resistance, and you have a polite obstinacy which makes me gently come to whatever you like. The frequent visits began, next came serenades and entertainments in their train, followed by presents. I opposed all that, but you are in no way rebuffed and step by step you are overbearing my resolutions. For my part, I can no longer answer for anything, and I believe that in the end you will make me come to matrimony, from which I have so held aloof.

DORANTE: Faith, Madame, you should already have been there. You are a widow, and depend only upon yourself. I am my own master and I love you more than my life. What reason is there that, from today on, you should not comprise all my happiness?

DORIMÈNE: O Heavens, Dorante, on both sides there must be a great many qualities to live happily together; and two of the most reasonable persons in the world often have difficulty in composing a union of which they are both satisfied.

DORANTE: You're jesting, Madame, to represent to yourself so many difficulties in it, and the experience you have had does not settle anything for everyone else.

DORIMÈNE: Well, I always come back to this. The expenses that I see you put yourself to for me disturb me for two reasons. One is, that they engage me more than I could wish; the other is, that I am sure—no offence to you—that you cannot do this without incommoding yourself, and I don't want that.

DORANTE: Oh, Madame, they are trifles, and 'tis not by that . . .

DORIMÈNE: I know what I'm saying; and among others, the diamond you forced me to take is of a value. . . .

DORANTE: Oh, Madame! For mercy's sake, don't place so much value on an object that my love finds unworthy of you, and allow. . . . Here's the master of the house.

SCENE XVI

(Monsieur Jourdain, Dorimène, Dorante, Lackey)

MONSIEUR JOURDAIN: *(After having made two bows, finding himself too near Dorimène).* A little farther, Madame.

DORIMÈNE: How?

MONSIEUR JOURDAIN: One step, if you please.

DORIMÈNE: For Heaven's sake, what?

MONSIEUR JOURDAIN: Step back a little for the third.

DORANTE: Madame, Monsieur Jourdain knows what's what.

MONSIEUR JOURDAIN: Madame, it is a very great honor to me to be so fortunate as to be so happy to have the joy that you should have had the goodness to accord me the graciousness of doing me the honor of honoring me with the favor of your presence; and, had I also the merit to merit a merit such as yours, and if Heaven . . . envious of my benefit . . . should have accorded me . . . the advantage of seeing me worthy . . . of the . . .

DORANTE: Monsieur Jourdain, that is sufficient. Madame does not love great compliments, and she knows that you are a man of wit. *(Aside to Dorimène)*. He's a good plain citizen, rather ridiculous, as you see, in all his ways.

DORIMÈNE: *(Aside to Dorante)*. It is not very difficult to perceive it.

DORANTE: *(Aloud)*. A gallant man, completely.

DORIMÈNE: I have great esteem for him.

MONSIEUR JOURDAIN: I have not yet, Madame, done anything to merit this favor.

DORANTE: *(Aside to M. Jourdain)*. Be careful, nonetheless, not to speak to her about the diamond that you have given her.

MONSIEUR JOURDAIN: *(Aside to Dorante).* Might I not merely ask her how she likes it?

DORANTE: *(Aside to M. Jourdain).* What? Take good care that you don't. That would be very vulgar of you; and, to act as a gallant man, it is necessary that you behave as though it were not you who made her that present. *(Aloud).* Madame, Monsieur Jourdain says he is delighted to see you at his house.

DORIMÈNE: He much honors me.

MONSIEUR JOURDAIN: *(Aside to Dorante).* How obliged I am to you, sir, for speaking thus to her for me!

DORANTE: *(Aside to M. Jourdain).* I have had the most frightful difficulty to get her to come here.

MONSIEUR JOURDAIN: *(Aside to Dorante).* I don't know how to repay you such favors.

DORANTE: Madame, he says that he thinks you the most beautiful woman in the world.

DORIMÈNE: He really renders me a favor.

MONSIEUR JOURDAIN: Madame, it's you who render favors, and . . .

DORANTE: Let's think about eating.

LACKEY: *(To M. Jourdain).* Everything is ready, sir.

DORANTE: Come, then, to sit down to table. And let the musicians be summoned.

(Six cooks who have prepared the banquet dance together, making the Third Interlude. After which they carry in a table covered with many dishes of food.)

ACT FOUR

SCENE I

(Dorimène, Monsieur Jourdain, Dorante, Three Musicians, Lackeys)

DORIMÈNE: Why, Dorante, that is an absolutely magnificent repast!

MONSIEUR JOURDAIN: You jest, Madame, and I would it were worthy of being offered to you. *(All sit down to table).*

DORANTE: Monsieur Jourdain is right, Madame, to speak in that way, and he obliges me in so well rendering you the honors of his house. I am in agreement with him that the repast is not worthy of you. Since it was I who ordered it, and since in this matter I do not have the accomplishments of our friends, you do not have here a very masterly meal, and you will discover incongruities of viands and some barbarisms of taste. If Damis had had a hand in it, everything would have been according to rule; throughout there would have been elegance and erudition, and he would not have failed to have emphasized the importance of all the dishes of the repast which he would have given you, and to make you agree to his great capacity in the science of good food; he would have told you of hearthstone bread, with its golden brown overlapping crust, tenderly crunching beneath the teeth; of a smooth, full-bodied wine, fortified with a sharpness that is not too predominant, of a loin of mutton gormandized with parsley, of a loin of veal *de rivière,* long as that, white, delicate, and which beneath the teeth is a veritable almond paste, of partridges heightened by a surprisingly flavorful sauce, and, for his *pièce de résistance,* a jellied consommé accompanied by a fat young turkey quartered with pigeons and surrounded by white onions alternated with chicory. But, for my part, I confess to you my ignorance; and, as Monsieur Jourdain has so well said, I could wish that the repast were more worthy to be offered to you.

DORIMÈNE: I make no reply to this compliment except by eating as I am doing.

MONSIEUR JOURDAIN: Oh! What pretty hands!

DORIMÈNE: The hands are mediocre, Monsieur Jourdain; but you mean to speak of the diamond, which is very beautiful.

MONSIEUR JOURDAIN: I, Madame? God forbid that I should care to speak of it; that would not be acting as a gallant man, and the diamond is a very trifling matter.

DORIMÈNE: You are very finical.

MONSIEUR JOURDAIN: You are too kind . . .

DORANTE: *(After signalling to M. Jourdain).* Come, let wine be poured for Monsieur Jourdain and for these gentlemen who are going to sing a drinking song for us.

DORIMÈNE: 'Tis marvellously to season the viands, by

mixing music with 'em, and I see I am being admirably regaled here.

MONSIEUR JOURDAIN: Madame, it's not . . .

DORANTE: Monsieur Jourdain, let us be silent for these gentlemen; what they have to say to us is worth more than anything we could say.

(The two male singers and the woman singer take the wine cups, sing two drinking songs, accompanied by all the instruments.)

FIRST DRINKING SONG

Drink a drop, Phyllis, start the glass round,
for a glass in thy hand doth have charms.
When I see thee together, O Bacchus and Phyllis—
—who each furnishes 'tother with arms—
my ardor for both doth compound.
So take we an oath, Phyllis, Bacchus, and I,
to love with a passion that never can die!

By wetting thy lips he receives added attractions,
while thy lips are by him beautified.
Oh, ye both make me yearn for ye,
and in long draughts I become drunk with ye!
So take we an oath, Phyllis, Bacchus, and I,
to love with a passion that never can die!

SECOND DRINKING SONG

Dear friends, let us drink, let us drink!
Time that flies invites us to drink!
Let us get out of life what we can,
for once crossed the Dark River's span,
it's goodbye to wine and to love.
So drink, now or never,
We can't drink forever.

Let fools do the reasoning
on what's the chief joy of life.
We find it 'mongst wine-pots, that's where!
Possessions and knowledge and fame
do not make us forget carking care.
How be happy in life?
To our way of thinking
'Tis found only in drinking.

Pour an extra round, boys, more, more, more.
Keep on pouring, boys, till they say, "We can drink no more!"

DORIMÈNE: I don't believe 'tis possible to sing better, and that is absolutely beautiful.

MONSIEUR JOURDAIN: I see something here, Madame, that is still more beautiful.

DORIMÈNE: Oh, là, là! Monsieur Jourdain is more gallant than I thought.

DORANTE: How now, Madame! What did you take him for?

MONSIEUR JOURDAIN: I wish she would take me for what I shall tell her.

DORIMÈNE: Again?

DORANTE: You don't know him.

MONSIEUR JOURDAIN: She may know me whenever it pleases her.

DORIMÈNE: Oh! I give up!

DORANTE: He is a man who always has a repartee handy. But do you not see, Madame, that Monsieur Jourdain eats all the pieces you have touched?

DORIMÈNE: I am carried away by this man, Monsieur Jourdain!

MONSIEUR JOURDAIN: If I could carry away your heart, I would be . . .

(Enter Madame Jourdain)

SCENE II

(Madame Jourdain, Monsieur Jourdain, Dorimène, Dorante, the Three Musicians, the Lackeys)

MADAME JOURDAIN: Oh, ho! I come upon fine company here, and I well see I was not expected. Was it for this pretty affair, Mr. Husband, that you were in such a hurry to send me to dine with my sister? I have just seen a theatre below, and here I find a banquet fit for a wedding. That's the way you spend our money, and thus you feast the ladies in my absence, and give them music and put on a comedy while you send me packing.

DORANTE: What do you mean, Madame Jourdain? And what fancies are these that you're getting into your head, that your husband spends his money, that it is he who is giving this entertainment to Madame? Know that it is I, pray; that he only lends his house to me, and that you should better consider the things you say.

MONSIEUR JOURDAIN: Yes, impertinent creature, 'tis the Count that presents all this to Madame, who is a person of quality. He does me the honor of taking my house and of wanting me to be with him.

MADAME JOURDAIN: All that is stuff and nonsense. I know what I know.

DORANTE: Madame Jourdain, put on, pray, better spectacles.

MADAME JOURDAIN: I don't need spectacles, sir, I see you clearly enough; for a long time I've sensed things, and I'm not a fool. This is very base of you, base of a great lord, to lend a hand as you do to the follies of my husband. And you, Madame, for a great lady, 'tis neither fine nor nice of you to place dissension in a household and to allow my husband to be in love with you.

DORIMÈNE: What does all this mean, for Heaven's sake? I must say, Dorante, it's the height of impertinence to expose me to the stupid fantasies of this absurd woman. *(She goes out)*.

DORANTE: Madame! Stop! Madame, where are you running?

MONSIEUR JOURDAIN: Madame! My Lord the Count, make excuses to her and try to bring her back. *(To Madame Jourdain)*. Oh! Impertinent creature that you are, these are fine doings of yours, to come to insult me in front of everyone and drive people of quality out of my house.

MADAME JOURDAIN: I don't care a rap for their quality.

MONSIEUR JOURDAIN: I don't know who holds me back, cursed woman, from splitting your head with the remains of the repast you came to disturb. *(The table is removed)*.

MADAME JOURDAIN: *(Going out)*. I don't care a rap for that. These are my rights that I'm defending, and I'll have all the wives on my side.

MONSIEUR JOURDAIN: You do well to avoid my fury. She came here most unfortunately. I was in the humor to say pretty things, and never had I felt so witty. But what's this?

(Enter Covielle, disguised)

SCENE III

(Covielle, disguised, Monsieur Jourdain, Lackey)

COVIELLE: Sir, I don't know whether I have the honor to be known to you?

MONSIEUR JOURDAIN: No, sir.

COVIELLE: I have seen you when you were no taller than that. (*Holding his hand a distance of one foot from the floor*).

MONSIEUR JOURDAIN: Me?

COVIELLE: Yes. You were the prettiest child in the world, and all the ladies took you into their arms to kiss you.

MONSIEUR JOURDAIN: To kiss me?

COVIELLE: Yes, I was a great friend of the late Monsieur Jourdain, your father.

MONSIEUR JOURDAIN: Of the late Monsieur Jourdain, my father?

COVIELLE: Yes. He was a very honorable gentleman.

MONSIEUR JOURDAIN: How did you say?

COVIELLE: I said that he was a very honorable gentleman.

MONSIEUR JOURDAIN: My father?

COVIELLE: Yes.

MONSIEUR JOURDAIN: Did you know him very well?

COVIELLE: Assuredly.

MONSIEUR JOURDAIN: And you knew him to be a gentleman?

COVIELLE: Without doubt.

MONSIEUR JOURDAIN: Then I don't know how the world is made!

COVIELLE: What?

MONSIEUR JOURDAIN: There are some stupid people who choose to tell me that he was a tradesman.

COVIELLE: He, a tradesman! 'Tis pure slander, he never was one. All that he did was that he was very obliging, very officious, and, since he was a connoisseur in stuffs, he went everywhere to choose them, had them brought to his house, and gave them to his friends for money.

MONSIEUR JOURDAIN: I'm delighted to make your acquaintance, so that you may testify to it that my father was a gentleman.

COVIELLE: I'll maintain it before everybody.

MONSIEUR JOURDAIN: Before everybody?

COVIELLE: Yes.

MONSIEUR JOURDAIN: You'll oblige me. What business brings you here?

COVIELLE: After having known the late Monsieur Jourdain, your father, honorable gentleman, as I told you, I have voyaged throughout the world.

MONSIEUR JOURDAIN: I imagine it's a long way in that country.

COVIELLE: Assuredly. I returned from all my long voyages only four days ago; and because of the interest I take in everything that touches you, I come to announce to you the best possible news.

MONSIEUR JOURDAIN: What news?

COVIELLE: You know that the son of the Grand Turk is here?

MONSIEUR JOURDAIN: Me? No.

COVIELLE: What! He has a magnificent retinue; everybody goes to see him, and he has been received in this country as a great lord.

MONSIEUR JOURDAIN: Forsooth, I did not know that.

COVIELLE: What is advantageous to you in this is that he is in love with your daughter.

MONSIEUR JOURDAIN: The son of the Grand Turk?

COVIELLE: Yes. And he wants to be your son-in-law.

MONSIEUR JOURDAIN: My son-in-law, the son of the Grand Turk?

COVIELLE: The son of the Grand Turk your son-in-law. As I went to see him, and perfectly understand his language, he conversed with me and, after other remarks, he said to me, "*Acciam croc soler ouch alla moustaph gidelum amanahem varahini oussere carbulath*"—that is to say, "Have you not seen a beautiful young person who is the daughter of Monsieur Jourdain, a Parisian gentleman?"

MONSIEUR JOURDAIN: The son of the Grand Turk said that of me?

COVIELLE: Yes. Seeing that I told him in reply that I

knew you particularly well and that I had seen your daughter, he said, *"Oh, Marababa sahem."* That is to say, "Oh, how enamored I am of her!"

MONSIEUR JOURDAIN: *"Marababa sahem"* means "Oh, how enamored I am of her"?

COVIELLE: Yes.

MONSIEUR JOURDAIN: Faith, you do well to tell me so, for as for me I would never have believed that *"Marababa sahem"* could have meant to say "Oh, how enamored I am of her!" What an admirable language is this Turkish!

COVIELLE: More admirable than one can believe. Are you aware of the meaning of *Cacaracammouchen?*

MONSIEUR JOURDAIN: *Cacaracammouchen?* No.

COVIELLE: It means: It means, "My dear soul."

MONSIEUR JOURDAIN: *Cacaracammouchen* means "My dear soul?"

COVIELLE: Yes.

MONSIEUR JOURDAIN: Why, that's wonderful! *Cacaracammouchen,* My dear soul. Would you ever suppose that? Why, I'm dumbfounded.

COVIELLE: In short, to finish my embassy, he comes to demand your daughter in marriage; and, so as to have a father-in-law who should be worthy of him, he wants to make you a *Mamamouchi,* which is a certain high rank in his country.

MONSIEUR JOURDAIN: Mamamouchi?[1]

[1] *This manufactured word means, according to Littré, "A goodfornothing."*

COVIELLE: Yes, *Mamamouchi;* that is to say, in our language, a Paladin. A Paladin, that's one of those ancient . . . Well! Paladin, there's nothing nobler than that in the world, and you will rank with the greatest lords of the earth.

MONSIEUR JOURDAIN: The son of the Grand Turk greatly honors me, and I pray you, take me to him, to express my thanks.

COVIELLE: What! He is on the point of coming here.

MONSIEUR JOURDAIN: He intends to come here?

COVIELLE: Yes. And he is bringing everything for the ceremony of your rank.

MONSIEUR JOURDAIN: Why, that is very hasty.

COVIELLE: His love will suffer no delay.

MONSIEUR JOURDAIN: All that perplexes me here is that my daughter is an obstinate piece who has gone and got into her head a certain Cléonte, and she swears she'll marry no man but that one.

COVIELLE: She'll change her opinion when she sees the son of the Grand Turk; and then, there happens a wonderful chance, here: it is that the son of the Grand Turk resembles this Cléonte almost exactly. I have just seen him, they showed him to me; and the love she has for the one may easily pass to the other, and . . . I hear him coming. There he is.

(Enter Cléonte)

SCENE IV

(Cléonte, as a Turk, with three Pages carrying his outer vestment, Monsieur Jourdain, Covielle, disguised.)

CLÉONTE: *Ambousahim oqui boraf, Jordina, salamalequi.*

COVIELLE: *(To Monsieur Jourdain).* That is to say: "Monsieur Jourdain, may your heart be all the year like a flowering rosetree." These are the fashions of speaking agreeably in those countries.

MONSIEUR JOURDAIN: I am His Turkish Highness's most humble servant.

COVIELLE: *Carigar camboto oustin moraf.*

CLÉONTE: *Oustin yoc catamalequi basum base alla moran.*

COVIELLE: He says that Heaven has given you the strength of lions and the wisdom of serpents.

MONSIEUR JOURDAIN: His Turkish Highness does me too much honor, and I wish him all kinds of prosperity.

COVIELLE: *Ossa binamen sadoc babally oracaf ouram.*

CLÉONTE: *Bel-men.*

COVIELLE: He says that you shall quickly go with him to prepare yourself for the ceremony, in order to see your daughter afterwards and conclude the marriage.

MONSIEUR JOURDAIN: So many things in two words?

COVIELLE: Yes, the Turkish language is like that, it says a great deal in a few words. Go quickly where he desires.

SCENE V

(Dorante, Covielle)

COVIELLE: Ha, ha, ha! Faith, that is absolutely funny. What a dupe! Had he learned his rôle by heart, he could not have played it better. *(Sees Dorante)*. Oh, ho! Pray, sir, kindly help us here in an affair that is taking place.

DORANTE: Ah, ha, Covielle, who would have recognized you? How you are decked out, fellow![1]

COVIELLE: You see, ha, ha!

DORANTE: What are you laughing at?

COVIELLE: At a thing, sir, that well deserves it.

DORANTE: How?

COVIELLE: I'll give you many times, sir, to guess the stratagem we are using with Monsieur Jourdain, to bring his mind to give his daughter to my master.

DORANTE: I do not guess the stratagem at all, but I guess it will not fail to have its effect, since you are undertaking it.

COVIELLE: I know, sir, that the animal is known to you.

DORANTE: Tell me what it is.

COVIELLE: Be so kind as to withdraw a little farther off, to make room for what I see coming. You can see a part of the affair, while I narrate the rest to you.

---

[1] *The word "fellow" is added by the translator to render the feeling of the familiar "tu" used by Dorante in speaking to the servant.*

(The Turkish ceremony for ennobling Monsieur Jourdain is performed in song and dance, and comprises the Fourth Interlude.)

FOURTH INTERLUDE

(The Mufti, Four Dervishes, Six Turkish Dancers, Six Turkish Musicians, and other instrumentalists dressed as Turks.)

(The Mufti invokes Mahomet with the twelve Turks and the four dervishes. After which, Monsieur Jourdain is brought in, dressed à la Turk, without turban or sword. To him the Mufti sings in a jabbered-French.[1])

MUFTI

If thou know'st,
Answer.
If not know,
Speak not, speak not.

Me be Mufti
Who be thee?
Thou not savvy?
Speak not, speak not.

[1] *The language is called in French "Petit-Nègre" and corresponds to "Pidgin English."*

(The Mufti, in the same jabbered-French, asks the Turks present to tell him what religion is Monsieur Jourdain's, and they assure him he is a Mohammedan. The Mufti invokes Mahomet in this lingua-franca, and sings the following words:)

MUFTI

Mahomet, for Jourdain,
I pray night and morning;
wanna make a Paladin
of Jourdain, of Jourdain.
Give him scimitar and give turban,
with galley-ship and brigantine
to fight for Palestine.
Mahomet, for Jourdain (etc.)

(The Mufti asks the Turks if Monsieur Jourdain will be firm in the Mohammedan religion, and sings to them:)

MUFTI

Will be good Turk, Jourdain?

TURKS

Yes, by Allah!

MUFTI

Hulaba, balachou, balaba, balada.

(The Turks repeat the same words.[1] The Mufti proposes to give the turban to M. Jourdain and sings as follows:)

[1] *Jabberwocky.*

MUFTI

You no rascal?

TURKS

No, no, no!

MUFTI

You no rogue?

TURKS

No, no, no!

MUFTI

Give the turban, give the turban.

(The Turks repeat what the Mufti says, to give the turban to M. Jourdain. The Mufti and the Dervishes put on their ceremonial turbans; the Mufti is presented with the Koran; he then makes a second invocation with all the other Turks present; after his invocation he hands a sword to M. Jourdain and sings these words:)

MUFTI

Thee be noble, and not be weak one.
Take the scimitar.

(The Turks repeat the same verse, all with scimitars in hand, pretending to give M. Jourdain saber-blows. The Mufti commands the Turks to give M. Jourdain a bastinado, and sings the following words:)

MUFTI

Give, give
the bastinado.

(The Turks repeat the same verse, giving him several blows, in rhythm.

The Mufti, after having punished M. Jourdain, sings the following to him:)

MUFTI

Don't be shamed;
This is the last affront.

(The Turks repeat the same verse.

The Mufti commences another invocation and withdraws after the ceremony with all the Turks, dancing and singing to the accompaniment of several Turkish instruments.)

ACT FIVE

SCENE I

(Madame Jourdaine, Monsieur Jourdain)

MADAME JOURDAIN: Oh, my Heavens! Mercy on us! What's all this? What a figure! Is it a masquerade you are going to wear, and is this a time to go masked? Speak, then! What is this? Who has bundled you up like that?

MONSIEUR JOURDAIN: See the impertinent woman, to speak in this way to a *Mamamouchi!*

MADAME JOURDAIN: What's that?

MONSIEUR JOURDAIN: Yes, you must show me respect now, for they've just made me a *Mamamouchi.*

MADAME JOURDAIN: What do you mean to say with your *Mamamouchi?*

MONSIEUR JOURDAIN: *Mamamouchi,* I tell you. I'm a *Mamamouchi.*

MADAME JOURDAIN: What animal is that?

MONSIEUR JOURDAIN: *Mamamouchi,* that is to say, in our language Paladin.

MADAME JOURDAIN: Paladin-baladin! Are you at an age to dance in the ballet?[1]

MONSIEUR JOURDAIN: What an ignorant woman! I said

[1] *In the original French, Madame Jourdain mistakes the word Paladin for Baladin, i.e., a strolling player.*

Paladin. It's a dignity of which they have just now gone through the ceremony.

MADAME JOURDAIN: What ceremony, eh?

MONSIEUR JOURDAIN: Mahomet-for-Jourdain.

MADAME JOURDAIN: What does that mean?

MONSIEUR JOURDAIN: Jourdain—that is to say, me, Monsieur Jourdain.

MADAME JOURDAIN: Well, so what, Jourdain?

MONSIEUR JOURDAIN: Wanna-make-a-Paladin of Jourdain.

MADAME JOURDAIN: What?

MONSIEUR JOURDAIN: Give-turban-with-galley-ship.

MADAME JOURDAIN: What's the meaning of that?

MONSIEUR JOURDAIN: To-fight-for-Palestine.

MADAME JOURDAIN: What in the world do you mean to say?

MONSIEUR JOURDAIN: Give-give-the-bastinado.

MADAME JOURDAIN: What's this jargon?

MONSIEUR JOURDAIN: Don't-be-ashamed-this-is-the-last-affront.

MADAME JOURDAIN: What the, what then, is all that?

MONSIEUR JOURDAIN: *(Dancing and singing). Hulaba, balachou, balaba, balada. (Tumbles to ground).*

MADAME JOURDAIN: Oh, Heavens, my husband has gone crazy.

MONSIEUR JOURDAIN: *(Getting up and going out).* Peace, insolent woman! Show respect to Sire Mamamouchi.

MADAME JOURDAIN: Where have his senses gone to? I must run to stop him from going out. Oh, ho! And here comes our last penny-piece![1] I see nothing but vexations on all sides.

(She goes out, as Dorante enters.)

SCENE II

(Dorante, Dorimène)

DORANTE: Yes, Madame, you are going to see the pleasantest thing that can be seen; and I don't believe it would be possible to find in all the world another man as insane as that one is. And also, Madame, we must try to promote Cléonte's amours by supporting his entire masquerade. He's a very gallant man and deserves our interest in him.

DORIMÈNE: I value him highly and he deserves happiness.[2]

DORANTE: In addition, we have a ballet which is return-

---

[1] *The French phrase "Voici justement le reste de notre écu" is no doubt a proverbial expression, used by money-changers. René d'Hermes suggests that its meaning may be "We lacked nothing more." We have taken it to refer to Dorante, who is entering, and who has milked Monsieur Jourdain of a great deal of money. Certainly the phrase is mistranslated in the Everyman's Library edition: "Here come the rest of our gang."*

[2] *In the seventeenth century, as today, the phrase "bonne fortune," is a context such as this, refers to "happiness in love."*

ing to us, and which we should not allow to be lost. And by all means it must be seen if my idea will succeed.

DORIMÈNE: I saw magnificent preparations there, and these are things, Dorante, that I cannot longer allow. Yes, I want to put a stop, at last, to your lavish spending; and to check the course of all these expenditures that I see you make for me, I have decided to marry you with dispatch. This is the real secret of it, and all these things end in marriage, as you know.

DORANTE: Oh, Madame! Is it possible that you should have taken such a sweet resolve for me?

DORIMÈNE: It is only to keep you from ruining yourself; otherwise, I plainly see that before long you would not have a penny.

DORANTE: How obliged I am to you, Madame, for the care you have to preserve my fortune! It is entirely at your service, as well as my heart, and you may use it in the way you like.

DORIMÈNE: I'll make use of them both. But here is your goodman: his costume is admirable.

SCENE III

(Monsieur Jourdain, Dorante, Dorimène)

DORANTE: Sir, we come to pay homage, Madame and I, to your new dignity, and to rejoice with you at the marriage you are concluding between your daughter and the son of the Grand Turk.

MONSIEUR JOURDAIN: *(After bowing in the Turkish manner).* Sir, I wish you the strength of serpents and the wisdom of lions.

DORIMÈNE: I was very glad, sir, to be among the first to come to congratulate you upon the high degree of glory to which you have risen.

MONSIEUR JOURDAIN: Madame, I wish your rose-tree to flower all the year; I am infinitely obliged to you for taking part in the honors that come to me; and I have great joy in seeing you returned here, so that I may make very humble excuses for the absurdity of my wife.

DORIMÈNE: That's nothing. I excuse such an impulse in her: your heart must be precious to her, and it is not strange that the possession of such a man as you are should inspire some alarms.

MONSIEUR JOURDAIN: The possession of my heart is a thing that has been entirely acquired by you.

DORANTE: You see, Madame, that Monsieur Jourdain is not one of those men that prosperity blinds, and that he knows how, in his glory, to know his friends, still.

DORIMÈNE: It is the mark of a completely generous soul.

DORANTE: Where is His Turkish Highness? As your friends, we would much like to pay our respects to him.

MONSIEUR JOURDAIN: There he comes, and I have sent to fetch my daughter to give him her hand.

SCENE IV

(Cléonte, Covielle, Monsieur Jourdain, etc.)

DORANTE: *(To Cléonte).* Sir, we come to bow before Your Highness as friends of the gentleman, your father-in-law, and to assure Your Highness, with respect, of our very humble services.

MONSIEUR JOURDAIN: Where's the interpreter to tell him who you are and to make him understand what you say? You'll see: he'll reply, and he speaks Turkish marvellously well. Ho, there! Where the devil has he gone? *(To Cléonte). Strouf, strif, strof, straf.* The gentleman is a *grande segnore, grande segnore, grande segnore.* And Madame is a *granda dama, granda dama.* Oof! He, Monsieur, he be *Mamamouchi,* French *Mamamouchi,* and Madame also French *Mamamouchi.* I can't speak more clearly. Good, here's the interpreter. Where are you going, you? We'll not know how to say a thing without you. Tell him, won't you, that the gentleman and lady are persons of great quality, who have come to pay their compliments to him, as my friends, and to assure him of their services. You'll see how he'll reply.

COVIELLE: *Alabala crociam acci boram alabamen.*

CLÉONTE: *Catalequi tubal ourin soter amalouchen.*

MONSIEUR JOURDAIN: Do you see?

COVIELLE: He says that the rain of prosperity waters the garden of your family in all seasons.

MONSIEUR JOURDAIN: I did tell you that he speaks Turkish!

DORANTE: That's admirable.

SCENE V

(Lucile, Monsieur Jourdain, Dorante, Dorimène, etc.)

MONSIEUR JOURDAIN: Come, my daughter; draw near and give your hand to the gentleman who does you the honor of demanding you in marriage.

LUCILE: Why, father! How you are got up! Are you playing a comedy?

MONSIEUR JOURDAIN: No, no, 'tis not a comedy, 'tis a very serious affair, and the most full of honor for you that could be wished. Here is the husband I bestow upon you.

LUCILE: Upon me, father?

MONSIEUR JOURDAIN: Yes, upon you. Come, give him your hand, and praise Heaven for your happiness.

LUCILE: No. I don't want to marry.

MONSIEUR JOURDAIN: Well, I, who am your father, want it.

LUCILLE: I won't do it.

MONSIEUR JOURDAIN: Oh! What a to-do! Come, I say. There, your hand.

LUCILE: No, father, I've told you, there is no power that can oblige me to take any husband other than Cléonte. And

I shall rather resolve myself to take all the extreme measures than to . . . *(Recognizes Cléonte)*. It is true that you are my father; I owe you entire obedience; and it is for you to dispose of me according to your wishes.

MONSIEUR JOURDAIN: Well! I am delighted to see you so promptly returned to your duty, and it truly pleases me to have an obedient daughter.

SCENE VI

(Madame Jourdain, Monsieur Jourdain, Cléonte, etc.)

MADAME JOURDAIN: How now? What's this? They say that you want to give your daughter in marriage to a Mardi-Gras mummer?

MONSIEUR JOURDAIN: Will you hold your tongue, saucy woman? You're always coming to bring your absurdities into everything, and there's no way to teach you to be reasonable.

MADAME JOURDAIN: 'Tis you that there's no way of making sensible, and you go from folly to folly. What is your plan, and what do you intend to do with this assemblage of people?

MONSIEUR JOURDAIN: I plan to marry your daughter with the son of the Grand Turk.

MADAME JOURDAIN: With the son of the Grand Turk?

MONSIEUR JOURDAIN: Yes. Pay your respects to him through that interpreter there.

MADAME JOURDAIN: I have no need of an interpreter; and I'll plainly tell him myself, to his face, that he shall certainly not have my daughter.

MONSIEUR JOURDAIN: Once more, will you hold your tongue?

DORANTE: What! Madame Jourdain, do you oppose such an honor as that? You refuse His Turkish Highness as son-in-law?

MADAME JOURDAIN: Heavens, sir, mind your own business.

DORIMÈNE: 'Tis a great glory, which is not to be rejected.

MADAME JOURDAIN: Madame, I pray you also not to trouble yourself with what does not concern you.

DORANTE: 'Tis the friendship we have for you that makes us take an interest in your advantages.

MADAME JOURDAIN: I can easily do without your friendship.

DORANTE: There's your daughter who agrees to the wishes of her father.

MADAME JOURDAIN: My daughter agrees to marry a Turk?

DORANTE: Undoubtedly.

MADAME JOURDAIN: She can forget Cléonte?

DORANTE: What does one not do to be a great lady?

MADAME JOURDAIN: I'd strangle her with my own hands if she had played a trick like that.

MONSIEUR JOURDAIN: Here's a great idle chatter. I tell you, this marriage shall take place.

MADAME JOURDAIN: And me, I tell you it shall not take place.

MONSIEUR JOURDAIN: Oh, what a din!

LUCILE: Mother!

MADAME JOURDAIN: Go, you are a hussy.

MONSIEUR JOURDAIN: What! Do you quarrel with her for obeying me?

MADAME JOURDAIN: Yes. She is mine as much as yours.

COVIELLE: Madame!

MADAME JOURDAIN: What do you want to tell me, you?

COVIELLE: A word.

MADAME JOURDAIN: I can do without your word.

COVIELLE: *(To M. Jourdain)*. Sir, if she would hear a word in private, I promise you to make her agree to what you want.

MADAME JOURDAIN: I'll not agree to it.

COVIELLE: Only listen to me.

MADAME JOURDAIN: No.

MONSIEUR JOURDAIN: Listen to him.

MADAME JOURDAIN: No, I don't want to listen.

MONSIEUR JOURDAIN: He will tell you . . .

MADAME JOURDAIN: I don't want him to tell me anything.

MONSIEUR JOURDAIN: There you have the great obstinacy of a woman! Will it hurt you to hear him?

COVIELLE: Only listen to me; afterwards you may do what you like.

MADAME JOURDAIN: Well, what?

COVIELLE: *(Aside to Madame Jourdain).* For an hour, Madame, we've been signalling to you. Do you not plainly see that all this is done only to adjust ourselves to the imaginings of your husband? That we are fooling him under this disguise and that it is Cléonte himself who is the son of the Grand Turk?

MADAME JOURDAIN: Oh, ho!

COVIELLE: And I, Covielle, am the interpreter?

MADAME JOURDAIN: Oh, then, I give up.

COVIELLE: Don't show anything.

MADAME JOURDAIN: Yes, 'tis done, I agree to the marriage.

MONSIEUR JOURDAIN: Ah! Now everyone's reasonable. You did not want to listen to me. I was sure he would explain to you what the son of the Grand Turk is.

MADAME JOURDAIN: He explained it nicely to me, and I am satisfied. Let us send to fetch a notary.

DORANTE: 'Tis very well said. And, Madame Jourdain, so that you may have your mind completely satisfied, and that you may lose today all the jealousy that you may have conceived of Monsieur Jourdain, your husband, we shall make use of the same notary to marry us, Madame Dorimène and me.

MADAME JOURDAIN: I agree to that also.

MONSIEUR JOURDAIN: *(Aside to Dorante).* It is to delude her into believing?

DORANTE: *(Aside to Monsieur Jourdain).* We must amuse her with this pretence.

MONSIEUR JOURDAIN: Good, good! Let someone go quickly to fetch the notary.

DORANTE: While waiting for him to come and while he draws up the contracts, let us see our ballet, and provide His Turkish Highness with the diversion of it.

MONSIEUR JOURDAIN: That is very well advised. Come, let us take our places.

MADAME JOURDAIN: And Nicole?

MONSIEUR JOURDAIN: I give her to the interpreter; and my wife to anyone that wants her.

COVIELLE: Sir, I thank you. *(Aside).* If there's a greater fool to see, I'll go tell it in Rome.

(The comedy ends with a ballet which has been prepared.)[1]

---

[1] *The ballet prepared by Lully was "A Ballet of Three Nations"—France, Spain, and Italy—in which songs were sung in the three languages. The story has no relation to the comedy of* Le Bourgeois Gentilhomme, *and the songs are merely, for the most part, songs of love.* *H.B.*